The Bridesmaid Handbook

A Helpful Guide for
Staying Organized
and Having Fun

BY HEATHER LEE
ILLUSTRATIONS BY AGNESBIC

CHRONICLE BOOKS
SAN FRANCISCO

Library of Congress Cataloging-in-Publication Data available.

ISBN 978-1-7972-0732-2

Manufactured in India.

Design by AJ Hansen and Rachel Harrell. Illustrations by Agnesbic.

10 9 8 7 6 5 4 3 2 1

Azazie is a registered trademark of Azazie Inc. AirBnb is a registered trademark of Airbnb Inc. BHLN is a registered trademark of BHLN LLC. Birdy Grey is a registered trademark of Birdy Grey. Bluetooth is a registered trademark of Bluetooth Sig, Inc. City Chic is a registered trademark of Ciy Chic. Craigslist is a registered trademark of Craigslist Inc. Facebook is a registered trademark of Facebook Inc. FaceTime is a registered trademark of Apple Inc. Fame and Partners is a registered trademark of Frilly Inc. Google Hangouts and Youtube are registered trademarks of Google Inc. Lulus is a registered trademark of Lulus. Paypal is a registered trademark of Paypal Inc. Plum Pretty Sugar is a registered trademark of Plum Pretty Sugar Inc. Show Me Your Mumu is a registered trademark of Show Me Your Mumu LLC. The Knot is a registered trademark of XO Group Inc. Venmo is a registered trademark of Paypal Inc. Vogue is a registered trademark of Conde Nast. Zoom is a registered trademark of Zoom Video Communications Inc.

Chronicle books and gifts are available at special quantity discounts to corporations, professional associations, literacy programs, and other organizations. For details and discount information, please contact our premiums department at corporatesales@chroniclebooks.com or at 1-800-759-0190.

Chronicle Books LLC
680 Second Street
San Francisco, California 94107
www.chroniclebooks.com

contents

She popped the question, and you said "Yes!"

You just agreed to be a bridesmaid. Now what?

Before you begin googling "bridesmaid duties" and "How much does being a bridesmaid cost?," take a deep breath and step away from the internet.

Chances are you've heard some wedding attendant horror stories. Maybe you've heard the one where the bride pressured a bridesmaid to pierce her ears in order to wear the earrings she was giving all the bridesmaids (because everything. must. match. perfectly.). Or the one where the bride ordered a bridesmaid's dress two sizes smaller to force her to lose weight (passive-aggressive, much?). Then there's the one where the bride requested that all the wedding party members stay behind to clean the reception venue (sweep, mop—all of it) after the party ended. Unfortunately, it seems like everyone knows someone who has a bad bridesmaid story, so it's no surprise you're wondering what you signed up for.

Saying yes to being a bridesmaid means taking on a major commitment for the next several months—one that comes with a lot of responsibility (not to mention out-of-pocket expenses). But at its core, the wedding attendant role is a beautiful representation of your relationship with the bride-to-be. She asked you to be a member of the wedding party because she loves you and wants you by her side on a very important day for her.

This book is a reference guide for bridesmaids, bridesmen, maids of honor, men of honor, and wedding attendants—basically, anyone who's been asked to be in the bridal party and is wondering what to do next. Whether you're looking for bridal shower–planning tips, a realistic breakdown of how much being a bridesmaid actually costs, or advice on how to make it through the wedding day with your friendship with the bride still intact, I hope this book becomes your go-to guide for all things bridesmaid.

So, buckle up, because being in the bridal party is going to be a wild ride. But I promise you that there is a way to not only make it through the experience but also have a genuinely amazing time—and you might not even have to wear an ugly dress.

CHAPTER ONE

Bridesmaids:
A Brief History

I f you've been asked to be a bridesmaid (or bridesman or wedding attendant, whichever term you prefer), there will be a moment when you take a step back and wonder to yourself: *Why do we even do this? Why do brides have bridesmaids, anyway? If it's "traditional," where did the tradition come from?*

Many wedding traditions and customs have changed over time (farewell, cringey garter toss!), yet having bridesmaids is a tradition that has endured. For the modern wedding, of course, there are duties that bridesmaids are supposed to help with, but beyond planning the bridal shower and standing by the bride's side during the ceremony, what's the story behind the lasting popularity of having bridesmaids? Interestingly, it seems that bridesmaids go pretty far back in history, with a number of possible origin stories explaining where the tradition comes from.

So here's a little backstory on the history of bridesmaids, how the role has changed over the years, and what it means for you.

Q: **Why do brides have bridesmaids?**

A: There are several popular bridesmaid origin stories. One of the most well-known dates back to the biblical story of Jacob. In recounting his marriages to Leah and Rachel, the story mentions that each bride was escorted by a female servant who was there to literally serve as her maid. And another: Ancient Roman law required ten attendants to be present for the wedding ceremony and serve as witnesses to make it official.

15

Bottom line

Although bridesmaids have always "served" the bride before and during the wedding, that does not make you her servant. You're her friend, first and foremost, and you were asked to be in the wedding party because of your close relationship. Trust me, it's very important to remember this.

Q: *Why do bridesmaids wear matching dresses?*

A: Believe it or not, the concept of matching bridesmaid dresses was not invented to make the bridesmaids look frumpy and thus the bride hotter by comparison. In fact, the tradition has a far more serious (and kind of creepy) origin story. Back in ancient Roman times, people believed that a happy occasion, such as a wedding, could attract evil spirits who might crash the wedding in an attempt to curse the bride and groom. To protect the bride, her bridesmaids were instructed to dress identically to her, basically acting as decoys so the spirits wouldn't be able to tell which woman was the bride. The evil spirits would become confused and their evil-doing plans would be thwarted, allowing the couple to marry.

In many cultures throughout history, brides presented their grooms with a dowry of money, jewelry, and other valuable goods, which made them targets for robbers (and jealous exes!). Again, the bride's dutiful attendants came to the rescue: Her bridesmaids wore similar outfits to befuddle the bandits so they wouldn't know who the actual bride was.

Over time, the role of bridal attendants has become less about risking your life for the bride and more about providing emotional support, as well as acting as a witness to the couple's union. The newlyweds might even ask you to serve as a witness to their marriage in an official capacity by signing the marriage license. (More on that, as well as other bridesmaid duties, a little later.)

Bottom line

If she hasn't initiated one already, have a conversation with the bride-to-be about what she's envisioning for her wedding attendants' attire. This is also a good time to have a candid conversation about your bridesmaid budget (learn more about budgeting in chapter five) and how much bridal party members might be spending on the various wedding-related festivities. Some questions to ask the bride: Will she be choosing the dresses/outfits? What does she have in mind? Or, would she prefer that the bridesmaids pick their own attire? If so, could she provide some guidelines to help narrow down the options? Here are some outfit ideas to consider together:

IDENTICAL DRESSES. This one is a little tricky to pull off, since everyone has a different style, personality, and body type. The key to success here is to choose a silhouette that all the attendants are happy to wear.

DIFFERENT DRESSES, SAME COLOR. The easiest way to make this option work is to choose one color and fabric type from one designer. Each bridesmaid can wear the selected color in a dress silhouette of their choosing—a style they feel comfortable and cute in.

SAME DRESS, IN TWO OR THREE COLORS. This is a solid option if the bride wants the wedding party to look coordinated but not overly matchy-matchy.

DIFFERENT DRESSES, SAME FABRIC/TEXTURE. Here, the bride chooses a specific type of fabric and lets each bridesmaid pick their own outfit accordingly. Some chic ideas: sequined dresses in a variety of metallic colors, lace dresses, or flowy, floor-length chiffon dresses.

DIFFERENT DRESSES IN THE SAME COLOR FAMILY. Stick with a color family (for example, shades of blue, metallics, earth tones) and select outfits in colors that jibe with the chosen palette. (Pro tip: Just be certain that once all the outfits are selected, the bride has time to see the looks together—cohesiveness is key here.)

JUMPSUITS. A jumpsuit is a great option if some wedding attendants would prefer to wear pants.

SUITS. Sleek, tailored menswear-inspired jackets and trousers for the entire bridal party is an edgy and super-stylish look.

PATTERNED DRESSES. Choose the same patterned dress for each person, or mix and match prints (everyone in mismatched florals, polka dots, stripes, etc.) that coordinate nicely together.

SEPARATES. Mix and match tops, skirts, and pants in complementary or matching colors.

PICK YOUR OWN DRESS. Some brides opt to give their attendants a little bit of guidance (for example, "wear something that will complement a beach setting") and then let them have free rein to wear whatever they'd like. Bonus: This option provides you with greater odds of wearing the dress or outfit again.

Q: Why am I not supposed to wear white (or can I)?

A: Weddings are synonymous with white bridal gowns, but white wedding dresses weren't the standard in the West until the 1800s, when Queen Victoria sparked the enduring trend by wearing one at her wedding to Prince Albert in 1840. By her side were her twelve bridesmaids, also clad in white.

As time went on, brides began to dress more elaborately than their bridesmaids, so the main goal of the bridesmaids' attire was not to outshine the bride's. The attendants were meant to look "charming, yet not too charming; distinctive, yet not too prominent," according to a 1920 issue of *Vogue*. Bridesmaids reverted to wearing colorful dresses, serving as a backdrop to the bride, resplendent in white. Thus we entered the era of the "bad" bridesmaid dress—frumpy frocks (think stiff taffeta, shiny satin, poufed sleeves) in garish colors that would be exiled to the back of the closet after one wear, never to see the light of day again.

21

As we've moved into the twenty-first century, pretty much anything goes when it comes to dressing the bridal party. Brides want their attendants to look as good as they do. Mix-and-match outfits and colors are now the norm rather than the exception, which means bridal parties are serving up looks that are chic and full of personality.

Bottom line

Brainstorm some wedding attendant outfit colors with the bride-to-be. Keep in mind that choosing a color for her attendants to wear can be a daunting decision, one of many the bride will need to make, so be patient and empathetic if your pal is experiencing decision fatigue. Here are some attire colors to consider:

- A color (or colors) that complements the wedding's overall color scheme, venue/setting, and season.

- Varying shades of one color (for example, shades of gray, ranging from dove gray and greige to charcoal). Pro tip: Stick to a palette of no more than three colors in

the same color family to keep the looks
coordinated and not chaotic.

- Black cocktail or floor-length dresses
  are an elegant choice for a more
  formal wedding.

- White bridesmaid dresses—à la Kate
  Moss and Kate Middleton—are chic again.

Q: *Why do bridesmaids carry bouquets?*

A: Today, brides and bridesmaids walk down the ceremony aisle carrying bouquets of popular flowers like garden roses, sweet peas, and peonies, but bridesmaid bouquets weren't always so pretty. During the Middle Ages, bouquets were less about favorite flowers and more about superstition. Bridesmaids carried bouquets of pungent spices and herbs, such as dill and garlic. The mix of strong-smelling elements (the stinkier, the better) was thought to keep evil spirits away so they couldn't curse the new couple with bad luck. (Are you sensing a theme? So many wedding traditions began as curse-prevention!)

Later, again inspired by the trendsetting Queen Victoria, who carried a bouquet of snowdrops (her husband-to-be's favorite flower) on her wedding day, brides and bridesmaids started carrying floral bouquets down the aisle. And though the bouquet toss is a tradition that many single bridesmaids dread, you might be surprised to learn about its origins. People used to believe that stealing a piece of the bride's wedding day attire would bestow some of her good fortune upon them (women would literally try to rip off a piece of her dress!). According to wedding lore, to escape from the crowd, the bride would toss her bouquet to create a diversion and then take off. Over the years, this act of distraction morphed into a tradition meant for a bride to pass on her good fortune; whoever caught the bouquet was thought to be the next lady in line to wed. Don't want to single out unmarried guests? Instead of the traditional bouquet toss, the bride can gift her bridal bouquet to the couple in attendance who has been married the longest as a celebration of their enduring love.

Bottom line

Skip the garlic-bulb bouquet and try one of these less pungent, more stylish options instead:

- A petite version of the bride's floral bouquet.

- An all-greenery bouquet with foliage like eucalyptus, ferns, or olive branches.

- A single, showy stem, such as a large peony blossom or a sculptural king protea.

- A small clutch or purse.

- A flower crown of fresh blooms to wear in your hair.

- A floral hoop "bouquet" made of a metal or wooden ring decorated with fresh flowers.

- A floral wrist corsage (If you're flashing back to the corsage you wore to prom, don't be alarmed—the couple's florist will make it look chic and stylish, promise!).

- Candlelit lanterns for a nighttime ceremony.

- Fans made of laser-cut wood, lace, paper, or painted silk; these are especially useful during a summer wedding or an outdoor wedding.

- Bridesmaids walking arm in arm with a groomsman/attendant instead of carrying a bouquet.

Q: Do the bride's attendants have to be female?

A: Let's face it, many wedding rules and customs are in serious need of a refresh, and this is one of them. Although wedding parties have historically been divided by gender—the bride was accompanied by her bridesmaids, and the groom was flanked by his groomsmen—couples today are choosing members of their wedding party based on their relationships with them, regardless of the person's gender. A wedding party can be comprised of bridesmaids, bridesmen, maids of honor, men of honor, groomsmen, groomswomen, best men, best women, wedding attendants, attendants of honor, and more. These options make a wedding party far more personal and a truer reflection of the couple and their closest relationships.

Bottom line

If you've been asked to be a bridesman or man of honor, congrats on being acknowledged as one of the bride's VIPs. There are a couple of logistical items you and the bride will need to consider. Be sure to talk about incorporating more guy-friendly party themes for the bridal shower and bachelorette party, as well as how to make sure your wedding day attire coordinates with the bridesmaids' attire (so that you're not mistaken for a groomsman). Also, discuss some ways you can be involved and helpful to her during the wedding planning process and on the actual wedding day.

CHAPTER TWO

Your Bridesmaid Bill of Rights

Being asked to be in a wedding is a big honor, but accepting a role in the wedding party also comes with great responsibilities (see a full list of what you're signing up for on page 53). Not only that, it's a commitment that will likely span anywhere from six to twelve months.

Considering what you're about to take on, it's important to establish some ground rules, or what I consider a Bridesmaid Bill of Rights (BBRs). These rules set healthy boundaries and help you know when to stand your ground.

BBR
#1: *You have the right to (kindly) say no.*

Agreeing to be in the wedding doesn't mean you're required to do the bride's bidding every minute of the day, and a wedding attendant should never feel obligated to do something that makes them feel uncomfortable. Here are some real-life situations you might find yourself in, as well as practical guidance on how to say no to them gracefully.

The situation:

Yes, you absolutely can say no to being in the wedding.

If you're reading this book, you've probably already agreed to be a bridesmaid. But, if you haven't given the bride your answer yet, or if you initially said yes but something legitimately came up (see below), then you are completely in the clear to kindly decline being in the wedding.

Legitimate excuses include (but are not limited to) the following:

YOU GENUINELY CANNOT MAKE IT TO THE WEDDING. How to say no: If you have already committed to an important event on the same day—something that cannot be changed—let the bride know ASAP. Be prepared for her to be disappointed, of course, but try to make it up to her by letting her know you will try your hardest to attend as many of the pre-wedding events and celebrations as possible.

YOUR FINANCES ARE SUPER TIGHT. How to say no: The unfortunate reality is that being a bridesmaid can be pricey. With outfits, multiple gifts, and possible travel to pay for, the expenses will quickly add up. If your current budget cannot accommodate the expenses that are associated with being in the wedding, then it's best to be completely honest with the bride. Explain your financial situation (you can be vague—you don't have to give her specific numbers) and then offer to be an extra set of hands whenever she might need some help: DIY-ing wedding favors, picking up out-of-town guests from the airport, or tying ribbons on ceremony programs are all great ways to pitch in. A good friend will understand and will not want her wedding to be a financial burden on you, especially if you are generous with your time and care for her. But in turn, be mindful of her feelings and refrain from instagramming your latest shopping hauls or tropical vacations—the bride might feel that you prioritized those things over being in her wedding.

YOUR SCHEDULE IS FULL. How to say no: Maybe you have a lot of work travel on the horizon. Perhaps you've already committed to being a bridesmaid in another wedding. Maybe you're planning your own wedding (congrats!). Or perhaps you're expecting a baby in the coming months (again, congrats!). Whatever the reason, if you're simply unable to commit to the time required to be a bridesmaid, then ultimately you're doing the bride a favor by declining, because no one wants a distracted wedding attendant. Be gentle when you explain your reasons to the bride, though, and make sure she knows you have her wedding date fully reserved in your calendar.

YOU DON'T FEEL CLOSE TO THE BRIDE. How to say no: This one's tricky, because it means the two of you aren't on the same page about the status of your friendship. Clearly, she feels a closer connection than you do, which is exactly why saying no in this situation, despite being incredibly hard, is absolutely the right thing to do. Being a bridesmaid purely out of obligation is going to end up being a burden, and who needs the extra stress and time commitment? Nip it in the bud and have what will surely be an awkward conversation with the bride.

Let her down gently and express that you're very honored to be asked, but that you have a lot on your plate in the coming months and don't feel able to put in the amount of effort required. Offer to help her with anything she might need along the way and be sure to buy the couple a really nice wedding present.

The situation:

Yes, you can say no to various wedding requests.

Even though it's hard to imagine ever saying no to your BFF, there might come a time when it's warranted. But here's the thing about saying no—you have to actually say it. Let the bride know ASAP that you can't accommodate her request—don't let the question remain unanswered for too long. For folks who are afraid of confrontation (me) and worried about disappointing others (also me), it sometimes feels easiest to simply not respond and hope they catch your drift. But trust me, avoiding the question is not the answer. Be direct, prompt, offer a brief explanation, and be kind.

With that in mind, here are some sticky situations you might encounter and how you can bow out of them while keeping your friendship intact:

YOU'RE UNABLE TO ATTEND ALL THE PRE-WEDDING EVENTS. How to say no: Even if you agreed to be in the wedding party, that doesn't mean you're required to attend every celebration leading up to the wedding (trust me, there are going be a lot of parties). You should make your very best effort to attend the bridal shower—that one's a biggie!—but if your schedule is hectic and/or your finances are tight, then it's perfectly acceptable to skip events where your attendance is less essential, such as a wedding dress–fitting appointment or even the bachelorette party (particularly if it involves airfare). Be up front with the bride from the get-go about possibly not making it to every pre-wedding event. And if you're unable to attend a particular occasion, let her know promptly and surprise her by sending a small gift, like a bottle of champagne and a sweet card explaining how disappointed you are to miss the event (you could arrange to have it waiting at the dress salon or in her hotel room for the bachelorette).

SAYING NO TO CERTAIN WEDDING REQUESTS.
How to say no: You might get a steady stream of small requests from the bride as plans for the wedding progress. These small asks can accumulate quickly, though, and soon they might feel big and burdensome. It could be buying a particular pair of heels to wear with the bridesmaid dress, or donning matching swimsuits for the bachelorette weekend in Palm Springs. Since expectations and emotions are running high during this time, it can be difficult for everyone involved to recognize whether a request is reasonable or not. You might think you should just grin and bear it, but biting your tongue repeatedly will ultimately lead to resentment. Instead, be authentic and honest, and gently let the bride know that you're having a hard time with certain requests. She cares enough about you to have included you in the wedding and should be willing to listen, empathize, and come to a compromise. Try not to minimize her request, and instead say something like, "I'm so excited about being in your wedding, but some of the things you're asking me to do are really difficult for me to manage."

#2: *You have the right to look and feel good on the wedding day.*

Sure, it's not your wedding day, but that doesn't mean you shouldn't look gorgeous too. The best way to guarantee that you actually like what you'll be wearing on the wedding day is to let the bride know you'd like to participate in the what-to-wear conversation.

Most brides will be elated that you'd like to be involved, so come prepared with inspiration photos of bridesmaid dresses and attendant outfits saved on your phone or Pinterest board. You could even take the extra step and research hair and makeup looks you like. Try to have this conversation as early as possible; basically, let her know from the get-go that you genuinely want to help take some of the load off her shoulders by helping her narrow down the outfit options. Do this as soon as you can, though—*before* the bride starts researching outfits on her own and bookmarking styles you would be bummed to wear. (Fair warning: Although most brides will appreciate your desire to be involved, some brides will prefer to decide on their own what their entourage will wear.)

In the same conversation, ask some questions about the bridal party's overall look. For example, if some members never wear dresses in real life, are jumpsuits, trousers, or suits an option? If someone doesn't usually wear makeup, do they have to get professional services on the wedding day? If an attendant has tattoos, is it fine if they're visible? If a bridesmaid isn't fond of strapless dresses, is one with sleeves an option? Don't make a fuss about minor details like colors or fabrics, but when it comes to important appearance and body-positivity issues, be sure to voice your concerns.

#**3**: You have the right to be treated as a friend (and not an actual maid).

Of course you want to participate and be as helpful as possible, but you don't want to be taken advantage of. Figuring out how to navigate the fine line between the two can be tricky. As a member of the bridal party, your main role is to provide the bride with moral and emotional support—not manual labor (even if the word "maid" is in your title). It is *not* your job to steam the wrinkles out of the table linens, watch YouTube videos to learn how to DIY flower arrangements, or break down the reception after the wedding is over. When a request from the bride (or the couple) veers into manual-labor territory and feels like, well, *just too much*—that's when you know it's time to set a boundary.

However, there are many tasks that are part of a bridesmaid's job description (keep reading, because we'll go into the full list of wedding attendant duties in chapters three and four): stuffing wedding invitations, holding the bride's dress while she uses the loo (sorry, there's no getting out of this one), hitting the dance floor to help get the party started (even though you hate dancing), being her on-call therapist when she needs a judgment-free vent session. And if you want to help out more than that? Go for it! But remember: You do not take the place of paid labor.

If you encounter a situation where you feel the bride is asking for too much, don't be afraid to sit down with her and gently let her know how you feel, whether it's anxiety about mounting expenses, requests that seem unreasonable, or simply feeling over-whelmed and stressed. Speak up as soon as you can (don't let your feelings fester and turn into resentment) and, as always, try to be kind. (See also BBR #1.)

43

BBR

#4: *You have the right to not go broke.*

It's no secret that being in a wedding party involves quite a few expenses. How much money should you expect to spend? That depends on your personal financial situation, of course, and we'll delve into budgeting in much more detail in chapter five. According to traditional wedding etiquette, it is customary for each attendant to cover the cost of their entire ensemble, from their attire to their accessories, hair, and makeup. Then, of course, there's getting yourself to and from the wedding, chipping in for the bridal shower and bachelorette, and various gifts along the way (I told you there were going to be a lot of parties!).

These days, however, there are ways for brides to lessen each attendant's financial burden. If they're willing and able, brides can offer to cover or contribute to the cost of their attendants' attire. Have a heart-to-heart discussion with the bride about the expenses wedding party members will be expected to cover, and ask if there's some flexibility in outfit styles and price points. Be sure to talk about accessories, hair, and makeup expenses as well. Chances are you already own a pair of shoes that will look great with the outfit, and maybe you'd prefer to handle your own hair and makeup rather than spend money on a pro. And if you can't afford a three-day weekend in Austin for the bachelorette, that's totally fine. Let the bride know by saying something like, "I wish I could go but I can't afford it right now, so I'm going to sit this one out. Have a great time and text me pics!" She'll be disappointed but, ultimately, she'll understand. The bottom line is no one should go into debt for being in someone's wedding. Every bride should be respectful of their attendants' budgets and the expenses they'll be paying for in order to participate in the celebration.

BBR
#5: *You have the right to bring a plus-one.*

Whether or not a couple should automatically give their wedding party members a plus-one is still a hotly debated topic. It shouldn't be. All wedding party members should be offered a plus-one.

Although it's understandable that a couple might need to keep a tight rein on their guest list—especially if they're on a strict budget and/or not including plus-ones for the rest of their guests—it's also important that wedding attendants be invited to bring a date, regardless of whether they're single, dating, partnered-up, cohabitating, married . . . whatever their love-life situation may be. It's just the right thing to do. Why? As one of their core wedding-team members, you're going to be expending a lot of time, energy, money, and emotional bandwidth throughout the entire wedding-prep process to help get the couple to the altar. Extending an invitation to bring a date to the wedding would be a small gesture of thanks for being so awesome.

What should you do if your wedding invitation doesn't include a plus-one? Rather than get mad, chalk it up to the bride mistakenly following some outdated wedding-etiquette advice. Talk to her directly and let her know that you're disappointed to not be offered a plus-one (and remember, your current dating status is irrelevant here). A thoughtful bride will quickly realize her error and fix the mistake. After all, you're a wedding VIP and should be treated like one.

Now that everyone has been given a plus-one, here are a couple of plus-one pointers to keep in mind:

- Your date is not free manual labor. No, your date is not going to pick up the ceremony chairs from the rental location and bring them to the venue. They're not going to help decorate the rehearsal dinner space, either. Partners of wedding attendants have to endure a lot: patiently listening to you vent when you feel over-whelmed or annoyed with the bride, not to mention a lot of awkward socializing while you're attending to your wedding party responsibilities. Even though it might seem as if your date is available to help with last-minute wedding errands, they are not required to do so. If your partner wants to offer their services to the couple, then congrats on finding an amazing person who is willing to go above and beyond the call of duty. But really, the only things your date needs to do are help you with any personal last-minute errands and be ready to boogie at the wedding.

- You and your date should be seated together at dinner. Although this one seems like a no-brainer, many couples decide to have a head table at the reception, where the newlyweds are seated at a long table, flanked by their wedding attendants. And sometimes, due to size limitations, the head table can accommodate only wedding party members and not their dates, who wind up being seated elsewhere (insert sad face). If possible, try to steer the bride away from the head-table concept so that wedding attendants can sit with their partners.

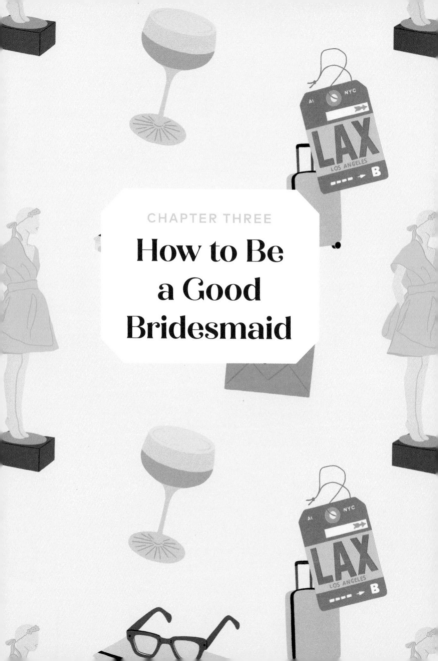

CHAPTER THREE

How to Be a Good Bridesmaid

Now that you're officially a brides-maid, what are you supposed to do, exactly? Being a good wedding attendant involves a whole lot more than just manicures and mimosas. But don't worry, your bride thinks you're the perfect person for the job. In this chapter, you'll find a comprehensive list of wedding attendant responsibilities—consider this your official get-her-to-the-altar guide.

If you've been asked to be the bride's honor attendant—a.k.a. the maid of honor, matron of honor, man of honor, best person, etc.—then skip ahead to chapter four on page 69 for a checklist that's tailored espe-cially for you.

Turn to page 215 for the Bridesmaid Duties: Setting Expectations worksheet. Designed for bridesmaids/attendants and the bride to fill out together, the worksheet will help set expectations and define the scope of your role.

Bridesmaid/Wedding Attendant Duties:
Before the Wedding

BE THERE FOR THE BRIDE. It's no secret that planning a wedding is a stressful under-taking, even for the most calm and collected of brides. A major responsibility as a member of her wedding crew is to lend an attentive ear and provide emotional support for her when she needs it. Let her vent her frustrations without judgment or interrup-tion, take her out for brunch when she needs a break from wedding planning, and cut her some slack when she's being a bit . . . *much*. In a nutshell, be a good friend to the bride.

BE THERE FOR THE MAID OF HONOR. The bride's honor attendant (maid of honor, matron of honor, man of honor, best person) will be responsible for all the duties on this list, and then some. So, a big task on your to-do list is to offer to help the maid of honor/honor attendant as much as possible and take some things off their plate. Also important: Don't assume that the maid of honor or other wedding party members will take care of the nitty-gritty details. Reach out and ask what you can help with; if there's nothing at the moment, offer to be on call for the next task that comes up.

HELP WITH WEDDING PLANNING TASKS (WITHIN REASON). Check in with the bride on a regular basis to see if she could use a hand with her wedding planning. Although you shouldn't be tasked with manual labor (as we discussed in chapter two), reasonable wedding planning tasks are fair game. Offer to research local cake designers. Send her a list of photographers your sister had considered for her own wedding last year. Brainstorm a slew of pun-tastic wedding hashtags. Let her know you'd be happy to book hotel rooms for out-of-town guests. Just be sure to set healthy boundaries so you aren't devoting every weekend to your bridesmaid responsibilities.

SET A BUDGET FOR YOURSELF. Once you've said yes to being in the wedding party, take a good look at your bank account and crunch the numbers to come up with what you're realistically able to spend on wedding attendant expenses. Create a budget and stick to it, and start saving each month to help lessen the strain on your wallet as the wedding gets closer. (We'll go over everything you should budget for in chapter five on page 98.)

GO WEDDING DRESS SHOPPING WITH THE BRIDE. Some brides want to shop with a gaggle of girlfriends, while others prefer a small group of two or three (some bridal salons may limit the number of companions a bride can bring to the salon). If you are invited to join, be honest about your thoughts on each dress, but be gentle. Encourage her to try on a variety of silhouettes; she may end up falling in love with a wedding dress style she hadn't previously considered. And if you aren't able to join the shopping excursion, ask a fellow bridesmaid to FaceTime you from the salon so you can watch the bridal fashion show.

HELP THE BRIDE SHOP FOR BRIDESMAID DRESSES/BRIDAL PARTY ATTIRE. Here's your chance to share any ideas you have about your own day-of attire with the bride, as discussed on page 17. But remember that the final decision is hers. If she chooses a dress or an outfit that is not your first choice, be gracious and enthusiastic about her decision (and attend all the fitting appointments, if necessary).

BUY YOUR BRIDESMAID DRESS/BRIDAL PARTY ATTIRE, SHOES, AND ACCESSORIES ON TIME. Be sure to order your wedding day ensemble as soon as you can so it arrives with plenty of time to spare. The last thing you want is for the style to sell out, forcing you to scramble for a backup plan. Spare yourself the stress by ordering your outfit and accessories promptly; this way, you'll still have time to squeeze in any alterations, if needed.

SPREAD THE WORD ABOUT THE COUPLE'S WEDDING REGISTRY. If the couple has a wedding website, they'll likely include their gift registry details on the site. But besides sharing the information online, the next best way to loop everyone in to the couple's registry is by word of mouth. The couple might ask you to help spread the word, so find out where they are registered so you can inform any friends or family members who might inquire.

RSVP FOR THE WEDDING AND OTHER EVENTS IN A TIMELY FASHION. Sure, she already knows you're coming, but it is good manners to formally RSVP. Plus, who doesn't love snail mail?

BOOK YOUR TRAVEL AND LODGING. If you'll be traveling to the wedding, the couple might have reserved a block of rooms at a few local hotels at a discounted rate. Act quickly to snag a reservation.

HELP PLAN THE BRIDAL SHOWER AND BACHE-LORETTE PARTY. Although the maid of honor/ honor attendant will likely take the lead, offer to handle some of the party-planning responsibilities. For example, you could volunteer to get pricing and capacity details for potential shower venues, or look up stylish Airbnbs for the destination bachelorette.

CONTRIBUTE FINANCIALLY TO THE PARTIES (WHILE STAYING WITHIN YOUR BUDGET). Have a candid conversation with the rest of the bridal party to discuss splitting the cost of all the pre-wedding parties. Review your personal finances in advance of the discussion to make sure your contribution is an amount you're comfortable spending.

ATTEND AS MANY PRE-WEDDING EVENTS AS POSSIBLE. Make it a priority to attend the bridal shower. As for the rest of the festivities, try your best to be a part of the bachelorette party, rehearsal dinner, and any other celebration, but be mindful of your own time and set limits on what you can commit to. If you're unable to attend an event, let the bride know as soon as possible.

BUY A WEDDING GIFT. You'll likely be buying several gifts for the bride over the course of her engagement, so be sure to budget accordingly. No wedding guest should show up empty-handed (and no, your presence doesn't count as a present). Find a gift on the registry that's within your price range (something small is perfectly fine) or go in on a larger gift with the rest of the bridal party.

GIVE A TOAST AT THE REHEARSAL DINNER. The bride's honor attendant will likely give a toast at the wedding reception, but that doesn't mean you can't also propose a toast to the newlyweds. The rehearsal dinner usually features a round or two of toasts by the couple's parents, close friends, and family members, so come prepared with a few heartfelt words to say.

Bridesmaid/Wedding Attendant Duties:

Getting Ready and Pre-Ceremony

PACK ALL YOUR WEDDING DAY NECESSITIES. Before you head to the getting-ready location, make sure you've packed everything you'll need to make it through the big day. You don't want to show up for hair and makeup only to realize you forgot to pack your heels.

Use our handy packing list on page 243 to ensure you've got everything covered.

ARRIVE AT THE GETTING-READY LOCATION ON TIME. This one's a biggie. It's imperative that you are punctual on the day of the wedding so that your hair and makeup (and the getting-ready photos) are completed on time. This ensures that the bride and her attendants will arrive at the ceremony venue with ample time to spare.

BRING SNACKS! It's going to be a long day, so make sure the bride and the rest of the bridal party are fueled up and well hydrated. Offer to do a coffee run before arriving for the hair and makeup session (you can take everyone's drink order at the rehearsal dinner the night before). Make sure the getting-ready room is stocked with a case of bottled water. Take the lead and coordinate a lunch delivery from a nearby café. And be sure to pack some of the bride's favorite treats for her to snack on while she's getting her hair done.

HELP THE BRIDE GET DRESSED. This task might require help from more than one bridesmaid, depending on the intricacy of the bride's wedding dress. It's also a lovely photo op.

Bridesmaid/Wedding Attendant Duties:
At the Ceremony

KNOW YOUR CUES. At the wedding rehearsal, you'll go over when you're supposed to walk down the aisle and where you should stand during the ceremony, so be sure to take note of your cues. If you're carrying a bouquet of flowers, hold the stems of the bouquet with both hands and keep your wrists near your hip bones. This position will keep your bouquet at the ideal height (it sounds weird but will look good in photos, I promise!) and will help you relax your shoulders.

KEEP AN EYE ON THE KIDS IN THE WEDDING PARTY. If there are little ones in the wedding party, you might need to watch over them to make sure they don't wander off before it's their turn to walk down the aisle. It's difficult for some kids to stay still and quiet for long periods of time, so don't be afraid to resort to bribery.

WALK DOWN THE AISLE DURING THE PROCESSIONAL. When it's your cue, walk down the ceremony aisle as the music plays in the background. Try to take it slow—there's no need to speed-walk down the aisle.

STAND BY THE BRIDE AT THE ALTAR. Remember that standing by your BFF's side during the ceremony is why you agreed to be a bridesmaid in the first place. Stand up straight, be fully present during this special moment for your friend, and, of course, smile.

EXIT THE CEREMONY DURING THE RECESSIONAL. After the "I dos," it's time to recess up the aisle and head to the reception to get the party started. For the recessional, you may be paired with another wedding attendant—together, you can link arms and walk up the aisle, toward the exit. Some couples will have a receiving line immediately following the ceremony, where the newlyweds, and sometimes wedding party members, stand outside the venue's front doors to greet guests as they exit.

GATHER YOUR AND THE BRIDE'S BELONGINGS AND BRING THEM TO THE RECEPTION. In the post-ceremony flurry, it's easy for things to get lost in the shuffle. Be sure to retrieve all your belongings and bring them to the reception; grab anything that belongs to the bride too.

Bridesmaid/Wedding Attendant Duties:
At the Reception

MINGLE WITH GUESTS. The newlyweds may not immediately make an appearance at the reception (they're probably signing the marriage license and posing for portraits), in which case it falls on the members of the wedding party to make sure guests are having a good time. Make an effort to introduce friends and family members of the couple who may be meeting each other for the first time.

PARTICIPATE IN THE GRAND ENTRANCE. Just before dinner is served, line up with your fellow wedding party members and wait for the emcee to announce you to the wedding guests as you enter the room. This is a high-energy moment, so stay pumped even if you might be a bit pooped!

SIT AT THE HEAD TABLE/YOUR ASSIGNED TABLE. During the cocktail hour, look at the seating chart to see where you and your date will be sitting for dinner, and take note of where the other bridal party members will be sitting in case you need to quickly find them.

ASSIST WITH WEDDING DRESS ADJUSTMENTS AND BATHROOM BREAKS. Yes, I'm talking about helping the bride pee in her wedding dress. Be the bride's fashion assistant when she needs to use the restroom, bustle her skirt, change outfits, or touch up her hair and makeup.

HIT THE DANCE FLOOR. Once the dance floor opens, it's time to get the party started. Grab your plus-one and hit the dance floor— if the wedding party looks like they're having a blast, other guests will soon follow.

MAKE SURE THE COUPLE EATS. The reception is arguably the most jam-packed portion of the celebration, and with the couple greeting all their guests, they might forget to eat. During cocktail hour, ask the wedding planner or a server to make up a plate of hors d'oeuvres for the couple to enjoy once they're done taking photos. And if it doesn't look like they'll be able to sit down and fully enjoy their entrées, ask them to also make two meal plates for them to eat later, when they have a moment to sit and catch their breath.

SEND OFF THE NEWLYWEDS IN STYLE. Your final task is to send the newlyweds off with a bang at the end of the night. Whether you decorate the getaway car with a trail of tin cans, pass out sparklers, or simply drive them straight to the airport to embark on their honeymoon, give the newlyweds a send-off they'll remember.

CHAPTER FOUR

How to Be a Good Maid of Honor

If you've been asked to be the bride's honor attendant—her maid of honor, matron of honor, man of honor, best person, etc.—congrats! Basically, you've been anointed by the bride to be her right-hand person, both literally and figuratively (you'll be the one to stand right next to her as she says "I do").

If you're not quite sure what to do next, especially if this is your first time being a member of a wedding party, then this chapter is just for you. While the previous chapter outlined a bridesmaid's responsibilities, as the bride's honor attendant, you'll be taking on all of those, as well as several additional key roles (marked with stars in the pages that follow). Brace yourself—it might initially feel like a lot. But I promise, not only will you be able to handle it all with style and grace, but also, by the end of the reception, you'll be crowned the wedding party MVP. Following is a list of everything you've been entrusted to do.

Turn to page 218 for the Maid of Honor Duties: Setting Expectations worksheet. Designed for the maid of honor/honor attendant and the bride to fill out together, the worksheet will help set expectations and define the scope of your role.

Maid of Honor/Honor Attendant Duties:

Before the Wedding

BE THERE FOR THE BRIDE. Planning a wedding is practically a full-time job, so it's no wonder your bride-to-be might seem a little stressed. Your main job as a wedding attendant is to support your BFF: Regularly check in with the bride to see how she's doing, and be a good listener if she needs to let off some steam (consider doing this over drinks, or sign yourselves up for a group kickboxing class—whichever is more her speed). In short, be extra generous and attentive to your friend.

69

★ **LEAD THE BRIDAL PARTY.** Being the bride's honor attendant means you're in charge of leading the rest of the bridal party throughout the planning process and on the day of the wedding. Take the lead in all things related to the bridal party: Be the one to initiate planning discussions, summarize email threads, assign tasks, and answer any questions the other attendants may have. And if a task comes up and it's unclear whose responsibility it is, assume it's yours and handle it yourself or assign the task to someone in the bridal party (in the least-bossy way possible, of course).

★ **BRING THE BRIDAL PARTY TOGETHER.** The bride will at some point introduce all the bridal party members to each other, but you should also take the initiative to connect the group. Whether you already know all the other attendants or have only met a few of them, it's important that everyone becomes acquainted well before the wedding day. Remember that you're the leader of this group, so the more you get to know each person, the more smooth and drama free the process will be. And since you'll need their help along the way—particularly when it comes to planning the bridal shower and bachelorette party—developing a friendly relationship is key. Here's how to break the ice and help everyone get to know each other:

• Start a group text. The first step is to initiate a group text with your fellow bridal party members. Although the bride may have already started her own text thread with all of you, it's important to have a separate group text she's not on, so everyone can openly discuss things like organizing the bridal shower and bachelorette. Begin the group text with a quick hello and an introduction;

encourage everyone to chime in and save each other's phone numbers.

- Plan a time to meet up in person. If some (or all) of the attendants are local, get a date on the calendar for everyone (including the bride) to hang out. Go out for drinks, meet at your favorite café, or make a reservation for brunch; just keep the vibe super casual so everyone can relax and get to know each other. If most of the bridal party members are located in far-flung places, organize a virtual night out via Zoom, FaceTime, or Hangouts, and encourage everyone to BYO their favorite cocktail to the online party.

★ GIVE EVERYONE IN THE BRIDAL PARTY A SAY.
Make sure everyone in the bridal party feels seen and heard. Take their opinions into consideration and let them know they can come to you directly with any questions, concerns, or ideas about anything, whether it's their thoughts about what they want to wear on the wedding day, budget boundaries, or bachelorette party activities. Encourage them to share ideas with you directly (rather than in a reply-all email, which can quickly become unmanageable); then you can jot

them down, filter out the ones you can answer, and bring the rest to the bride when she has less on her plate.

★ **LEAN ON YOUR FELLOW BRIDESMAIDS FOR HELP.** Even though you're the maid of honor, you do not have to be in charge of everything, always. Delegate tasks to your fellow attendants; for example, when planning an event like the bachelorette party, reach out to the others and assign each person an activity or a meal to be in charge of. And follow up midway to make sure everything is on track (again, without being bossy).

HELP WITH WEDDING PLANNING TASKS (WITHIN REASON). Offer to help check things off the bride's to-do list. It's best to play to your strengths: If you're a whiz at Excel, you could create a detailed guest-list spreadsheet so the couple can track each guest's name, mailing address, party size, RSVPs, gifts received, and menu selection. Did you go to law school? Let her know that you're happy to review her vendor contracts before she signs on the dotted line. Just be sure to set healthy boundaries for yourself and your time—don't forget that you've got a life of your own outside of helping plan your best friend's wedding.

* **DISCUSS FINANCES WITH THE GROUP AND SET A BUDGET FOR YOURSELF.** Have a candid conversation with the rest of the bridal party to discuss splitting the costs of all the pre-wedding parties. Don't assume everyone has an unlimited budget to spend or that everyone can pitch in the same amount; attendants on tighter budgets can offer to contribute in nonmonetary ways, like taking on more party planning, tackling DIY projects, or helping with setup and cleanup. Also, be sure to take a good look at your own finances to see how much you can realistically afford to spend. As the maid of honor/honor attendant, you might find yourself spending on little things here and there throughout the wedding adventure, and those items can quickly add up. Set a budget for how much you can spend per event and stick to it. (We'll go over everything you should budget for in chapter five on page 98.)

* **COORDINATE CALENDARS.** Before deciding on dates for the bridal shower and bachelorette party, ask the bride for a list of dates she'll be available. Then, send out an online survey to the bridal party so you can figure out when the most people will be available to attend.

GO WEDDING DRESS SHOPPING WITH THE BRIDE. The maid of honor/honor attendant is one of the chosen few who get to go wedding dress shopping with the bride, so mark the salon appointments on your calendar because these are do-not-miss events. Be patient, as shopping might involve a slew of appointments, and give honest but tactful feedback about each dress. Encourage the bride to try on a variety of silhouettes; she may end up falling in love with a style she hadn't previously considered. And when she emerges from the fitting room wearing *the one*, stand up and cheer!

HELP THE BRIDE SHOP FOR BRIDESMAID DRESSES/BRIDAL PARTY ATTIRE. Now's your opportunity to share with the bride those outfit inspiration photos you've collected and online shopping links you've saved. This is also the time to relay any fashion ideas and suggestions from the other bridal party members. Be vocal about what you'd like to wear but remember that, ultimately, it's her decision. And be kind and gracious about whatever winds up being her final choice, even if it wasn't your first pick.

BUY YOUR BRIDESMAID DRESS/BRIDAL PARTY ATTIRE, SHOES, AND ACCESSORIES ON TIME. Order your wedding day ensemble as soon as it's selected so it arrives with plenty of time to spare. You don't want to run the risk of the style selling out, forcing you to scramble for a backup outfit. Also, ordering the outfit promptly gives you time to have alterations made, if needed.

SPREAD THE WORD ABOUT THE COUPLE'S WEDDING REGISTRY. The couple might enlist you to help spread the word about their gift registry. In case any friends or family members ask, it's important that you know where the couple has registered so you can direct guests to the right place.

RSVP FOR THE WEDDING AND OTHER EVENTS IN A TIMELY FASHION. Of course, the bride already knows that you'll be at the wedding, but it is good manners to properly RSVP to the invitation.

BOOK YOUR TRAVEL AND LODGING. If you're traveling to the wedding, take advantage of the hotel-room block. Most couples will reserve a block of hotel rooms at a discounted group rate for their guests. The number of discounted rooms are usually limited, though, so book early to take advantage of the cheaper rate.

★ **TAKE THE LEAD IN PLANNING THE BRIDAL SHOWER AND BACHELORETTE PARTY.** As the maid of honor/honor attendant, you're expected to be at the helm for planning both the bridal shower and the bachelorette party, but don't be afraid to ask for (lots!) of help. Ask the other attendants to handle some of the party-planning details and divvy up the responsibilities. If someone is a great baker, put them in charge of the dessert table for the bridal shower. If someone is a crafty DIYer, ask them to create a colorful backdrop for group photos. Not only does this help everyone feel included, but also a lot more can be accomplished working as a team.

For a full rundown on how to plan these pre-wedding parties, see chapter six: How to Plan a Bridal Shower (page 113) and chapter seven: How to Plan a Bachelorette Party (page 155).

★ **FIND OUT WHAT KIND OF PARTY THE BRIDE REALLY WANTS FOR HER SHOWER AND BACHELORETTE.** Before you jump into party-planning mode, reach out to the bride to find out what she'd really like for her bridal shower and bachelorette party (don't just assume she'll be down with drunken debauchery). Some brides might say they trust you to throw a fabulous party they'll love, while others might like to have some input. It's OK to keep some details a surprise, but if the bride says no strippers, respect her wishes.

Have a chat with the bride to figure out what she really wants for her shower and bachelorette. Use the worksheets on page 222 (bridal shower) and page 225 (bachelorette party) to guide your conversation.

★ **KEEP THE PEACE.** Try your best to mediate any personality conflicts in the bridal party. Avoid taking sides, and try to get the individuals involved to resolve their differences and/or come to a compromise. If possible, don't involve the bride (she's already got a lot on her plate), but if you find yourself in an uncomfortable situation, where neither party is responding or cooperating, it's definitely OK to ask her to help defuse the situation.

ATTEND AS MANY PRE-WEDDING EVENTS AS POSSIBLE. The other attendants get a bit of a pass here, but as the honor attendant, you should really make it a priority to attend all the pre-wedding parties—most importantly, the bridal shower and the bachelorette. But be mindful of your own time and set limits on what you can commit to. If you're unable to attend an event, let the bride know as soon as you can.

BUY A WEDDING GIFT. No wedding guest should show up empty-handed (and no, your presence doesn't count as a present). Choose a gift from the registry that's within your price range (something small is perfectly fine) or arrange to go in on a larger gift with the rest of the bridal party.

★ **WRITE YOUR WEDDING TOAST.** Toasting the newlyweds is another special responsibility that's reserved for the bride's honor attendant. Don't wait until the last minute to write your speech—give yourself plenty of time to brainstorm ideas and practice your toast.

For tips on how to write and deliver a memorable wedding toast, read our speech-writing guide on page 202.

★ **CREATE A WEDDING DAY EMERGENCY KIT.** Be prepared for any wedding day mishaps by putting together an emergency kit filled with essentials like safety pins, ibuprofen, bandages, hair ties, and other items someone might need in a pinch.

Find a checklist of everything to put in your indispensable wedding emergency kit on page 244.

★ **MAKE A GETTING-READY PLAYLIST.** Surprise the bride by creating the perfect hair-and-makeup soundtrack for the morning of the wedding. Set the mood in the getting-ready suite with a combination of upbeat tunes and songs that will keep the bride relaxed as she prepares for her walk down the aisle.

Maid of Honor/Honor Attendant Duties:
Getting Ready and Pre-Ceremony

PACK ALL YOUR WEDDING DAY NECESSITIES. Give yourself plenty of time to pack everything you'll need for the wedding weekend. The big day will be a flurry of activity, and the last thing you want is to realize you've forgotten something and have to make a last-minute dash to the store.

Use the wedding day packing list on page 243 to ensure you've got everything you need for the wedding.

ARRIVE AT THE GETTING-READY LOCATION ON TIME. This one is nonnegotiable. It's important that you are punctual on the day of the wedding so that the hair and makeup session, and the getting-ready photos, can be completed on time, and everyone can head to the ceremony venue with ample time to spare.

BRING SNACKS! It's going to be a long day, so make sure the bride and the rest of the bridal party are fueled up and well hydrated. Offer to bring coffee to the hair and makeup appointment (you can take everyone's drink order at the rehearsal dinner the night before). Make sure the room is stocked with a case of bottled water, and coordinate a lunch delivery from a nearby café. A thoughtful touch: Pack some of the bride's favorite treats for her to snack on.

HELP THE BRIDE GET DRESSED. This task might require several members of the bridal party, depending on the intricacy of the wedding dress. Plus, it's also a lovely photo op.

★ **KEEP THE BRIDAL PARTY ON SCHEDULE.** On the day of the wedding, help make sure everything is running smoothly and according to schedule—in particular, the bridal party's hair and makeup appointments. Bring a printout of the wedding day schedule for easy reference, and if the couple has a wedding planner, periodically send them a quick text message with status updates.

Maid of Honor/Honor Attendant Duties:
At the Ceremony

* ★ **BRING A FEW JUST-IN-CASE TISSUES.** Before the ceremony begins, fold a few tissues into small squares and wrap them around the stems of your bouquet (if you're carrying one) or tuck them in your pocket in case anyone sheds happy tears during the ceremony.

* ★ **HOLD THE WEDDING RING.** The bride might ask you to hold her spouse-to-be's wedding ring during the ceremony. Then, you'll be asked to pass it to the officiant for the couple's ring exchange. If your outfit doesn't have pockets, you could discreetly carry it in a small jewelry pouch, or it might be simplest to have her partner's honor attendant carry both sets of rings (especially if they have pockets!).

KNOW YOUR CUES. You'll go over when you're supposed to walk down the aisle, as well as where you'll stand during the ceremony, at the wedding rehearsal (typically held the day before the wedding). Make a mental note of your exact spot to ensure the spacing between the wedding party members is even and looks good in the photos.

★ **DO A FINAL WEDDING DRESS CHECK FOR THE BRIDE.** Just before the processional begins, do a final check to make sure the bride's wedding dress, train, veil, hair, and makeup are perfect. Give her a kiss on the cheek!

WALK DOWN THE AISLE DURING THE PROCESSIONAL. When it's your turn, walk down the aisle at a slow and steady tempo. This will feel much slower than your normal walking pace, but trust me—it will help build anticipation for the bride's entrance to follow.

★ **STAND NEXT TO THE BRIDE AT THE ALTAR.** Remember that standing right next to the bride is an honor—stand up straight, be fully present during this major moment for your best friend, and, of course, smile.

★ **HOLD THE BRIDE'S BOUQUET.** When the officiant asks the couple to join hands, reach for the bride's bouquet and hold it during the vow and ring exchange. You can either hold both bouquets (yours and the bride's) or, if hers is huge, pass yours to the next bridesmaid. Handing off your bouquet leaves you with one hand free in case you need to fluff or adjust the bride's train. When the vows are done and she's ready to walk up the aisle, hand the bouquet back to her for the ceremony exit.

EXIT THE CEREMONY DURING THE RECESSIONAL. After the "I dos," it's time to recess up the aisle and head to the reception to get the party started. For the recessional, you may be paired with another wedding attendant—together, you can link arms and walk up the aisle, toward the exit. Some couples will have a receiving line immediately following the ceremony, where the newlyweds, and sometimes wedding party members, stand outside the venue's front doors to greet guests as they exit.

★ **SIGN THE MARRIAGE LICENSE.** Can I get a witness? Most states require one or two witnesses to be present for the wedding ceremony and, once it's concluded, to also witness the couple and officiant signing the marriage license. Then, it's the witnesses' turn to sign the document. Many couples ask their honor attendants to be their official witnesses, which means your signature helps make it legal and will be on their marriage license for posterity.

GATHER YOUR AND THE BRIDE'S BELONGINGS AND BRING THEM TO THE RECEPTION. In the post-ceremony flurry, it's easy for things to get lost in the shuffle. Be sure to retrieve all your belongings and bring them to the reception; grab anything that belongs to the bride too.

Maid of Honor/Honor Attendant Duties:
At the Reception

★ **HELP WRANGLE GUESTS FOR GROUP PHOTOS.** Trying to gather family members for group pictures after the ceremony can get hectic. Give the photographer a hand by grabbing all the right people for each shot (and tracking down anyone who might have wandered off).

★ **HOLD THE BRIDE'S PURSE.** During cocktail hour, offer to hold on to her clutch for safekeeping while she greets guests. When the reception begins, place it on the bride's chair at her dinner table.

MINGLE WITH GUESTS. It may take a while for the newlyweds to make an appearance at the cocktail hour (they're probably posing for portraits). Members of the wedding party should circulate among the guests and make an effort to introduce friends and family members of the couple who may be meeting each other for the first time.

PARTICIPATE IN THE GRAND ENTRANCE. Just before dinner is served, line up with your fellow wedding party members and wait for the emcee to announce you to the wedding guests as you enter the room. This is a high-energy moment, so stay pumped even if you might be a bit pooped!

SIT AT THE HEAD TABLE/YOUR ASSIGNED TABLE. During cocktail hour, take a look at the seating chart to see where you and your date will be sitting for dinner. Take note of where the other bridal party members will be sitting in case you need to quickly find them.

★ **GIVE A TOAST DURING DINNER.** Bring the house down with a killer wedding toast that includes all the reasons why you love the bride and why the newlyweds are perfect together. Keep it short—two to three minutes, max—and don't forget to bring a glass of champagne with you to the microphone!

For tips on how to write and deliver an epic wedding toast, read our speech-writing guide on page 202.

ASSIST WITH WEDDING DRESS ADJUSTMENTS AND BATHROOM BREAKS. Yup, I'm talking about helping the bride pee in her wedding dress. Be the bride's fashion assistant when she needs to use the restroom, bustle her skirt, change outfits, or touch up her hair and makeup.

HIT THE DANCE FLOOR. Once the dance floor opens, help get the party started. Find your plus-one and head out on the dance floor—if the wedding party looks like they're having fun, other guests will soon follow.

★ **KEEP AN EYE ON THE GIFTS.** The couple might ask you to take care of wedding gifts and cards they may have received that day. That could mean dropping everything off after the wedding, either at the couple's home or at their parents' place, so they can open them when they return from their honeymoon.

★ **DISTRIBUTE VENDOR GRATUITIES.** If the couple has a wedding planner, they will likely handle this task. If they don't, you might be asked to distribute any remaining final payments or gratuities to vendors at the end of the evening.

SEND OFF THE NEWLYWEDS IN STYLE. Home stretch! Your last task of the night is to organize a celebratory send-off for the newlyweds at the end of the reception. Coordinate with the other bridal party members on a grand departure, whether that's with sparklers, bubbles, noisemakers, or a trail of tin cans (empty White Claws, anyone?) attached to their getaway car.

CHAPTER FIVE

Bridesmaid Budget Breakdown

You might be eager to dive right into your wedding attendant responsibilities and start crossing things off your list, but pump the brakes for a second and slow down. Before you create that Pinterest board called "Bridesmaid Lewks," let's talk money. It's probably the least-fun aspect of being in a wedding, but setting a realistic budget for yourself and sticking to it is the best way to make sure you don't go into debt for your friend's wedding.

While you might be aware there are some costs associated with being in a wedding party, just how expensive is it to be a bridesmaid? According to data from The Knot, a popular wedding planning website, being a bridesmaid/wedding attendant can cost more than $1,700.

So how much money should you budget for your role in your bestie's wedding? And how much of that figure should be dedicated to your outfit, gifts, the bridal shower, bachelorette party, and the myriad other expenses that pop up? Although there is no one-size-fits-all budget, there are some helpful guidelines to follow as you whip out your calculator and assess your bank account. Following is a primer for planning your bridesmaid budget. Note: These costs are calculated in US dollars.

How to Create a Bridesmaid Budget

Set yourself up for financial success by figuring out what you can afford to spend and staying on top of all your expenditures along the way. Here are six steps to create (and stick to) a bridesmaid budget. Because—repeat after me: I'm not going broke for someone else's wedding.

1. START SAVING IMMEDIATELY.

Right after the bride asks you to be in the wedding, begin putting money aside on a weekly basis for wedding-related expenses. If possible, have the funds automatically transferred each week to a savings account (you could even name the account "Bridesmaid Fund") that is separate from your regular savings account. This way, you can watch the balance grow (so satisfying!), and you'll know exactly how much you have available to spend on wedding items.

2. FIGURE OUT WHAT YOU CAN AFFORD TO SPEND (BEFORE YOU START SHOPPING).

Before you begin ordering bridesmaid dresses, you'll need to know how much you can spend. The budget breakdown in the following section (page 97) provides an overview of all the attendant expenses you should expect to pay for. Take a look at your personal finances and determine what you can realistically afford to spend on each item. Jot those numbers down—that's your budget and you should aim to stay within that price range.

Turn to the Wedding Budget worksheet on page 236. Use it to create a budget, keep track of purchases, and stay on budget.

3. DISCUSS EXPENSES WITH THE BRIDE.

Now that you have a good sense of what your budget looks like, the next step is to figure out what the bride is going to cover and what you'll be paying for yourself. Have an honest conversation with her about money soon after you are asked to be in the wedding (it's much easier to have a heart-to-heart talk about costs before the receipts start piling up). She might bring it up first, but if she doesn't, you can broach the (super awkward, I know) topic by saying something straightforward, such as "I'm looking at my budget for the next few months and wanted to chat about bridesmaid expenses." And if you know your budget is going to be tight, let the bride know your limitations and that you might not be able to participate in every single wedding event. She'll understand. I promise.

4. TRACK YOUR EXPENSES ON A WORKSHEET.

Once you start making purchases related to the wedding, keep tabs on your spending by logging each expense on a worksheet or spreadsheet. Compare the amount you actually spent to the amount you had budgeted for the item. This will help prevent you from overspending on your bridesmaid obligations.

Don't forget to use the Wedding Budget worksheet on page 236 to track your expenses.

5. BUDGET FOR BIG-TICKET ITEMS FIRST.

Some bridesmaid/wedding attendant expenses are unavoidable: the dress/outfit and accessories, plane tickets to the wedding, and gifts, to name a few. These essential items are also the priciest, so budget for these first. Once these expenses are out of the way, it'll be easier to manage your money on smaller expenses like bridal shower decorations or matching swimsuits for the bachelorette.

6. DON'T FEEL PRESSURED TO SPEND MONEY YOU DON'T HAVE.

If you can't afford something, a straight-forward "that's beyond my budget right now" is all you need to say. If you are continually being put in uncomfortable situations where you feel pressured to spend more than your bank account says you can, reconsider participating in the bridal party. A true friend will not want you to go into debt for their wedding.

BRIDESMAID

BUDGET

BREAKDOWN

Here's a real-talk look at what you should expect to spend as a bridesmaid.

WHAT TO BUDGET FOR:
YOUR WEDDING DAY LOOK

One of your biggest expenses will be your wedding day look. This includes the bridesmaid dress/attendant outfit, as well as some extras you might not have initially thought of, such as alterations, undergarments, and hair styling and makeup services on the wedding day.

BRIDESMAID DRESS/ ATTENDANT OUTFIT

WHO PAYS: The bridesmaid/attendant. Most often, the attendant covers the cost of their outfit for the wedding day, though in some (rare) cases,

the bride may decide to purchase outfits for the bridal party as a gift.

EXPECT TO PAY: $100–$300

HOW TO SAVE: She picks the colors, you pick the outfit. This option is the easiest on a bridesmaid's wallet, so try to nudge the bride in this direction. If she chooses a particular color palette, then everyone can buy a dress or an outfit they like in those hues. This way, you'll have lots of flexibility to choose a style that's not only within your budget but also may be something you'll want to wear again.

Buy used or rent whenever possible. Be sure to browse resale sites like eBay, thredUp, Tradesy, and Poshmark. Many former bridesmaids sell their dresses to recoup some cash, so you might be able to score the perfect dress secondhand and in great (a.k.a. no one will ever know) condition. Another money-saving option is to skip the outfit purchase altogether and rent a style from a service like Rent the Runway.

Think out of the box. You might not consider H&M or ASOS as go-to bridesmaid dress/outfit resources, but these fast-fashion retailers usually carry many options that would work perfectly for a wedding. Keep a close watch on these sites—you and the rest of the wedding party crew could nab a seriously stylish outfit for less than $100. Other online retailers to keep tabs on: BHLDN, Show Me Your Mumu, Azazie, City Chic, Birdy Grey, Fame and Partners, Plum Pretty Sugar, and Lulus.

ALTERATIONS

WHO PAYS: The bridesmaid/attendant

EXPECT TO PAY: $50–$200

HOW TO SAVE: Make it work. Ideally, the goal would be to find a dress or an outfit that fits you perfectly—no alterations necessary. If your dress requires some very minor adjustments, you might be able to get away with DIY-ing them yourself. If a dress strap needs to be shortened, turn the dress inside out and pin the excess with a safety pin. If the hem needs to be shortened just a touch, use hem tape or try on a pair of higher heels to see if the proportions work better.

Find your own tailor. For trickier alterations, you'll need to call a pro. Ask around for tailor and seamstress recommendations; having the alterations done by a local small business instead of the dress salon is almost always cheaper.

UNDERGARMENTS

WHO PAYS: The bridesmaid/attendant

EXPECT TO PAY: $25–$50

HOW TO SAVE: Wear something you already own. Fingers crossed the outfit the bride wants you to wear doesn't require having to fork over additional cash for a specialty undergarment. But if the style is, say, a backless dress and you don't already own a pair of adhesive "chicken cutlets," then you might have to spend money on a good backless bra.

SHOES AND ACCESSORIES/JEWELRY

WHO PAYS: It depends. Attendants typically pay for their own accessories, but if the bride is asking you to wear specific shoes, shawls, or jewelry, she might purchase them herself and give those items as a gift. Every bride is different, though, so it's best to assume you're on your own until you hear otherwise.

EXPECT TO PAY: $50–$200 (shoes), $50–$200 (accessories/jewelry)

HOW TO SAVE: Shop your closet. Before spending any money on new accessories, try shopping your own closet—you might unearth a cute clutch you had forgotten about or a pair of heels you haven't worn in ages but happen to be the perfect shade of gold.

Borrow from a friend. Chances are many of your pals are on the wedding circuit too, which means they might have some stylish accessories, such as purses, jewelry, or shoes, that they've worn to previous weddings and could kindly lend to you.

Buy used. Secondhand and vintage stores are great spots to find inexpensive clutches and costume jewelry.

HAIR, MAKEUP, AND MANICURE

WHO PAYS: It depends. These primping obligations can sometimes cause tension, especially if the bride isn't up front about who will be paying for them. Among wedding-industry pros, there are different schools of thought on who should pick up the tab for the bridesmaids' hair and makeup. Some think the services should be the bride's treat, especially if she wants everyone to have their hair and makeup done professionally. Others say each attendant should cover their own services—it's part of the bridesmaid gig. Whichever camp your bride is in, it's best to assume that you'll be paying for your hair, makeup, and manicure. And if the bride says later that she'd like to pay for the services, awesome! If she doesn't, no biggie— you've already set aside funds for them, so you are well prepared.

EXPECT TO PAY: $100–$200

HOW TO SAVE: Do your own hair and makeup. If you or another wedding attendant are skilled at doing hair and/or makeup, then skip the pro services. Just be sure to confirm with the bride that she's cool with it, and build plenty of time in the wedding day schedule so that you won't have to rush. Also, a trial run is always a good idea!

Choose a simpler style. If the bride wants everyone to have their hair and makeup done by the same team, then pricing will likely vary according to each person's specific styling needs. Choose a simpler look that's quicker to execute—makeup is sometimes cheaper without adding false eyelashes, and "down" hairstyles are typically more affordable than updos.

Do your own nails. Many brides schedule a group outing to a nail salon before the wedding for a little spa time with their bridal party. If your budget is tight, do your nails at home but meet the gang at the salon so you can still be a part of the festivities.

WHAT TO BUDGET FOR:
THE WEDDING DAY

Be sure to factor in everything you'll need to get yourself to the wedding, as well as at least two nights' of accommodations: the night before the wedding and the night of the wedding (because you'll need a place to crash after the after-party).

TRAVEL TO THE WEDDING

WHO PAYS: The bridesmaid/attendant

EXPECT TO PAY: $50–$1,000. Depending on whether you're driving or flying, this could be anywhere from $50 for gas to $1,000 or more for a flight to an international destination, plus a rental car or taxi rides.

HOW TO SAVE: Book your travel early. Begin looking for flights at least four months in advance and be on the lookout for airfare deals and sales.

Split the cost. Coordinate your travel plans with other bridal party members and split a rental car to save on transportation expenses.

ACCOMMODATIONS

WHO PAYS: The bridesmaid/attendant. In most cases, the wedding party members are responsible for their lodging the night before and the night of the wedding. However, if the bride wants her whole squad to stay together the night before, she should cover the cost.

EXPECT TO PAY: $0–$800 for two nights ($0–$400 per night). If you live near the event venue, then lodging won't be a factor, unless you prefer to book a hotel room to be closer to the action.

HOW TO SAVE: Take advantage of the room block. Usually the couple will reserve a block of hotel rooms at a discounted group rate for their guests. Keep in mind there are usually a limited number of discounted rooms, so book early to take advantage of the cheaper rate.

Bunk up. If you're traveling to the wedding, see if any fellow out-of-town bridal party members or guests are interested in sharing a hotel room with you.

Go in on a house rental. Instead of booking separate hotel rooms, find a house that the bridal party can rent together for the weekend. Browse sites like Airbnb and VRBO to find a place that's large enough to accommodate everyone and is centrally located; splitting a house is usually more affordable than paying for individual hotel rooms.

WHAT TO BUDGET FOR:
GIFTS

You might feel the urge to buy a fancy gift for your BFF to mark each pre-wedding milestone, such as the engagement party and bridal shower, but pace yourself—you'll be spending a lot of cash leading up to the wedding, so stick to your budget and don't be tempted to overspend on presents.

ENGAGEMENT GIFT

WHO PAYS: The bridesmaid/attendant. Engagement gifts are optional; however, if the couple is throwing an engagement party, then it's a nice gesture to give them a gift, even if it's a modest one, so that you don't show up empty-handed.

EXPECT TO PAY: $30–$75

HOW TO SAVE: Keep it simple. Give the couple something to mark the occasion: a fancy bottle of bubbly, a pretty ring dish for the bride's new sparkler, a personalized hanger for the wedding dress, or a framed photo of the bride and her partner, paired with a thoughtful, handwritten card.

BRIDAL SHOWER GIFT

WHO PAYS: The bridesmaid/attendant. In case you are wondering, the answer is yes: Bridesmaids/attendants still need to give a bridal shower gift even though they're paying for the cost of the shower (more on this later).

EXPECT TO PAY: $50–$100

HOW TO SAVE: Give a group gift. Keep costs low by chipping in for a bridal shower gift with the rest of the bridal party.

WEDDING GIFT

WHO PAYS: The bridesmaid/attendant

EXPECT TO PAY: $100–$300

HOW TO SAVE: Shop the registry early. Once the couple has finished putting together their gift registry, jump online to get first pick of the gifts. Don't procrastinate; if you wait too long, the registry will be picked over and the only gifts left may be the pricey, big-ticket items. Shop early so you'll have plenty of presents to choose from in the price range that fits your budget.

Create a themed gift. Personalize your gift by pairing a smaller item from the registry with something you've hand-picked for them. For example, purchase the roasting pan they requested and pair it with your favorite cookbook—complete with sticky-note bookmarks on your favorite recipe pages. Or, if they registered for a set of six whiskey glasses, you could purchase two (leaving the rest for another guest to buy), and gift them with a bottle of your favorite bourbon.

Pitch in with others for a larger gift. Instead of an individual present, go in with the other bridal party members on one of the more expensive presents from their registry.

WHAT TO BUDGET FOR:
THE BRIDAL SHOWER

The bridesmaids/ attendants are usually in charge of planning and hosting (a.k.a. paying for) the bridal shower, though in some cases, the bride's mother or another relative may also jump in to plan and pay. If a family member offers to host the bridal shower, they will take on the costs, but the bridal party members should offer to contribute in some form, whether it's sharing expenses, helping prepare food, or setting up.

Find everything you need to know to plan an awesome shower in chapter six: How to Plan a Bridal Shower (page 113).

TRAVEL TO THE SHOWER

WHO PAYS: The bridesmaid/ attendant

EXPECT TO PAY: $0–$500. If you live nearby, travel expenses won't be a factor, of course, but if you have to travel to attend the shower, you could be spending anywhere from $50 on gas to $500 or more for a cross-country flight, taxis, and lodging.

HOW TO SAVE: Attend virtually. If you live out of town and your budget is very tight, everyone will understand if you can't make it to the bridal shower (just be prepared for the bride to be a bit disappointed). Let the bride and the other attendants know as soon as possible that you can't attend, and offer to help in any way they need. And, if you can swing it, let them know you're happy to chip in for some of the shower costs (this is a kind gesture but isn't expected). On your end, join the bridal shower via FaceTime, Hangouts, or Zoom so you can be a part of the celebration; download a bridal shower–themed background to use as your virtual party backdrop, and show up onscreen with a cocktail in hand. One caveat, though: If you are the maid of honor/honor attendant, you should really make every effort to attend the bridal shower in person.

SHOWER CONTRIBUTION

WHO PAYS: The bridesmaid/attendant

EXPECT TO PAY: $50–$200

HOW TO SAVE: Get involved. Since you'll be contributing to the party costs, get involved in the planning process so you can have a say in the overall budget.

Borrow from friends. Save on buying decorations by seeing what you can borrow from pals—it's bridesmaid season for some of them too, and they might have leftover or spare decorations you can borrow.

Shop secondhand. Remind yourself to periodically check Craigslist and Facebook Marketplace for lightly used decor items like cake stands and flower vases.

Speak up. Typically, bridal shower costs are split evenly among the members of the bridal party. However, if your finances are tight, let the maid of honor/honor attendant know ahead of time how much you're able to contribute and explain that you're happy to put in more party-planning legwork to help offset any difference. Offer to coordinate the guest list, order and send the invitations, plan the menu, show up early to help set up, and stay afterward to clean up.

WHAT TO BUDGET FOR:
THE BACHELORETTE PARTY

Bachelorette parties come in all sorts of shapes and sizes, from the more traditional "night on the town" featuring dinner, drinks, and dancing (and some debauchery, of course) to a multi-night bachelorette vacation in a far-flung tropical destination. Whatever your bride wants to do, keep in mind that bachelorette expenses can rack up quickly, so it's important to budget accordingly.

You'll find a stress-free guide to planning a bachelorette party the bride will remember forever in chapter seven: How to Plan a Bachelorette Party (page 155).

TRAVEL TO THE BACHELORETTE PARTY

WHO PAYS: The bridesmaid/attendant

Expect to pay: $0–$1,000. Travel costs for the bachelorette depend on whether the celebration will be held locally, or if it will be held out of town and will require airfare and other transportation expenditures.

HOW TO SAVE: Stay local. If you and the bridal party are on a tight budget, skip the destination bachelorette and plan a party close to home. Eliminating travel and accommodation costs will save everyone a lot of money.

Pass on this party. If you simply can't afford it, it's totally fine not to attend the bachelorette (especially if you've already attended other pre-wedding parties). Just be honest with the bride and the other attendants about your budget, and offer to take the bride for a local night out instead.

BACHELORETTE PARTY CONTRIBUTION

WHO PAYS: The bridesmaid/ attendant

EXPECT TO PAY: $50–$1,500. Again, this depends on how big of a bash you're throwing, so the amount can vary greatly. Typical costs might include your dinner and drinks, plus a portion of the bride's, if you're planning a night on the town, and lodging, transportation, entertainment, and additional meals if you're staying in a hotel or rental home for the weekend.

HOW TO SAVE: Agree on spending limits. Before you start planning the bachelorette, have a discussion with the rest of the bridal party about how much everyone feels comfortable spending on the party. Costs can accumulate quickly (drinks! a stripper! nightclub cover charges! pool floaties!), so see if everyone can come to a consensus. Be sure to factor in the party guest list, because all the attendees should split the costs evenly (unlike the bridal shower, the bridesmaids/attendants are not expected to cover this party).

Ask the bride to contribute. This one might sound like a major faux pas, but if you are planning a destination bachelorette, it is perfectly appropriate to ask the bride to chip in here and there, like in covering her travel costs (for example, her flight or a portion of the hotel or house-rental fee). Some groups decide to chip in for an evening out rather than pay for her entire stay. Just be sure to clearly communicate what the bridal party and other guests should expect to cover and what the bride should handle herself.

Wear something you already own. If possible, find something in your closet to wear to the bachelorette. But if you tossed out your clubbing clothes a long time ago, then buy something fun, cute, and, most importantly, cheap, because someone will definitely spill alcohol on it.

Ready to create your wedding budget? Turn to the Wedding Budget worksheet on page 236 to get started.

CHAPTER SIX

How to Plan a Bridal Shower

ext up on your wedding attendant to-do list: Plan an epic bridal shower for your BFF that she'll remember forever. I get it—that's a tall order, considering everything else you've got on your plate (you still have your own life to live, after all). But by following the planning guide in this chapter, and doing some heavy leaning on your fellow bridal party members for help, you'll be able to pull off a fabulous fête that she won't stop talking about. Keep reading for everything you need to know about hosting a bridal shower that's one for the books.

The bridal shower: FAQs

Let's start with some bridal shower basics. Here's every question you may have about this pre-wedding party, along with answers to help you take the celebration from just good to great.

WHAT IS A BRIDAL SHOWER? A bridal shower is a fun, festive gathering of the bride's close friends and family members to celebrate her upcoming marriage and spend quality time with her before the big day. It's also an opportunity for guests to "shower" the bride with gifts to help her set up her new home with her spouse. Traditionally, bridal shower attendees were exclusively women, but these days the guest list can include anyone the bride would like to invite, regardless of gender.

WHAT USUALLY HAPPENS AT A BRIDAL SHOWER? Bridal showers usually follow the same general format: food, drinks, mingling, games, gift opening, and dessert. The celebration sometimes concludes with the bride's spouse-to-be showing up at the party toward the end as a surprise. You should by all means feel free to mix things up in any way you think the bride would like. If she'd rather do a group activity, you could book a pasta-making or flower-arranging class; if she loves the great outdoors, maybe a group hike and picnic lunch would be right up her alley. If the idea of opening gifts in front of everyone makes the bride feel uncomfortable, then skip that part; she can open the gifts at home (find other gift-opening alternatives on page 138).

But before you begin planning the shower, consult with the bride about the kind of bridal shower she wants and what her expectations are for the celebration. To help guide that conversation, have her to fill out The Bridal Shower: Setting Expectations worksheet on page 222, which outlines all the important questions.

WHO PLANS AND PAYS FOR THE BRIDAL SHOWER? The bridesmaids/attendants are usually in charge of planning and hosting (a.k.a. paying for) the bridal shower. The maid of honor/honor attendant should take the lead in planning the shower, but decisions should be made collectively. Tasks and responsibilities should be divvied up as equally as possible so that everyone is able to contribute.

In some cases, the bride's mother, the bride's partner's mother, or another relative may jump in to plan and pay for the shower; however, this is the exception, not the expectation. If a family member does offer to serve as host, they will take on the costs, but the bridal party members should offer to chip in in some way, whether it's monetarily, helping prepare food, or setting up. If the bride's partner's mother doesn't live near where the bridal shower will be held, she may want to host and pay for a separate bridal shower for her future daughter-in-law. It's also common to have multiple bridal showers to accommodate loved ones in different states or locations. Also, the bride's coworkers may throw her a shower; those are typically organized and paid for by her work colleagues.

WHO'S INVITED? A bridal shower is usually a fairly intimate celebration, so guests should be limited to the bride's closest friends and family members. Ask the bride to provide you with a list of guests she'd like to invite, along with each person's email and snail-mail address. If the shower is going to be a surprise, the maid of honor/honor attendant should check in with the bride's mother and come up with a guest list together that they think the bride will be happy with.

MAKE SURE THE GUEST LIST MEETS THE FOLLOWING CRITERIA:

- Don't invite anyone who isn't also invited to the wedding. This one might seem a little obvious, but inviting someone to the bridal shower who isn't invited to the wedding is not a good look and comes off as being gift-grabby. The only exception:

a work bridal shower thrown by coworkers who want to celebrate the bride and share their well wishes (regardless of whether they are invited to the wedding or not).

- Each guest should be invited to only one shower. If the bride is having multiple bridal showers, guests should not receive invites to every shower. (Again, this isn't a gift-grab.) If there's any guest list overlap, it should be limited to bridal party members, mothers, and siblings, but they are not expected to attend more than one shower.

- Extend the courtesy invite. In almost every case, the following people need to be on the invitation list: mothers of the bride and groom/partner, sisters of the bride and groom/partner, and bridal party members. It's also a nice gesture to invite close friends or relatives of the bride who live out of town; they may not attend, but inviting them shows that the bride cares about them.

WHEN SHOULD YOU HOLD THE BRIDAL SHOWER? Usually the bridal shower is held three weeks to three months before the wedding. There's no hard-and-fast rule for choosing a party date, though—the best approach is to first ask the bride to share a couple of dates that work for her. Then, take a poll among her VIPs (most likely the bridal party members and her mom) to see which date works best for everyone. The goal is to choose a date that's convenient for the bride and her core party people, and this might mean hosting the shower a little further in advance of the wedding, planning it to coincide with the bride's next trip home, or combining it with another get-together, such as the bachelorette party (more on this in the next Q&A).

If possible, though, try to space out the timing of the bridal shower and bache-lorette party to give you and the rest of the bridal party enough time to plan and save for both events. Once the date has been selected, make sure the bride and her partner have put together their wedding registry before the invitations are sent out so guests can purchase gifts.

CAN YOU COMBINE THE BRIDAL SHOWER WITH THE BACHELORETTE PARTY? Of course! For some situations, it might be more conve-nient for the bride and many guests to have both the bridal shower and bachelorette party on the same day. That way, folks can set aside a full day to spend with the bride, and out-of-towners won't need to make two separate trips (which can be a costly and arduous endeavor). For example, friends and family members could gather at 1:00 p.m. for a bridal shower brunch; afterward, the bride and her pals can be picked up by a car service or limo for the bachelorette's night out on the town—dinner, drinks, and dancing. Check with the bride to see if a bridal shower/bachelorette combo is something she'd prefer.

SHOULD THE BRIDAL SHOWER HAVE A THEME?
It doesn't have to, but it certainly can! Having a party theme can help streamline many party-planning decisions, from the menu to the decorations and gifts. Turn to page 127 for some favorite bridal shower themes that are actually fun (read: not cheesy).

WHERE SHOULD YOU HOLD THE BRIDAL SHOWER?
If the bride lives relatively close to her hometown, then it's best to hold the bridal shower there. If she lives in another state, it may be simplest for the bride to travel to her shower if most of the guests

live locally, instead of asking everyone on the guest list to hop on an airplane. But if the guest list spans many different cities, states, and even countries, then it might make the most sense to have multiple showers. Maybe a bridesmaid who lives near the bride would like to host a local shower, while the bride's sister might want to host another shower closer to where the bride's family resides. Her partner's family may also want to host a bridal shower for their side of the family in another location. If that's the case, then the maid of honor/honor attendant should help coordinate the guest list for each occasion to make sure there isn't any accidental overlap (again, with the exception of mothers, siblings, and bridal party members).

The specific location depends on the type of shower and the host's budget. It could be in a friend or family member's home or backyard, at her favorite brunch spot, an events space, or somewhere more specific if the shower has a theme (such as a cooking school or a wine bar).

WHEN SHOULD BRIDAL SHOWER INVITATIONS BE SENT OUT? The invitations should be sent out six to eight weeks before the bridal shower, either by snail mail or email. Give guests a sneak peek at the celebration to come by choosing a design that complements the shower's theme or aesthetic. The invitation should include the bride's name, shower date and time, location, registry information, the name(s) of the host(s), how to RSVP, and the RSVP deadline (the date should be two to four weeks before the party). RSVPs can be collected via phone or email; there's no need for a printed RSVP to be sent back in the mail.

WHO SHOULD SEND THE INVITATIONS? The host of the bridal shower usually sends the invitations, but the host might decide to delegate this task to someone in the bridal party. For example, if the bride's aunt has offered to host the celebration, she might enlist party-planning assistance from bridal party members. The maid of honor or another attendant can offer to help with the invitations and assist with tasks ranging from getting the official guest list from the bride to ordering and mailing out the invites to keeping track of RSVPs as they come in. Be sure to include the point person's name and contact information (phone number and/or email address) on the invitation so guests can reach them directly with their RSVP.

Bridal showers should ideally last between two and four hours. Anything shorter and guests might feel like they didn't have a chance to spend time with the bride; anything longer and they'll be antsy to head home. Three hours is the perfect sweet spot. If your bride-to-be is shy, she might prefer a shorter shower (being in the spotlight for several hours can be draining). If this sounds like your bride, plan for two and a half to three hours. Also, be sure to list the start time and end time on the invitation so guests know in advance just how long the party will be.

What's a couple's shower?

These days, when it comes to weddings, almost anything goes. Couples are giving wedding traditions they feel are outdated a twenty-first-century update. Enter the couple's shower: Instead of a girls-only afternoon focused solely on the bride, a couple's shower is a joint celebration of both partners where all of their nearest and dearest—regardless of gender—are invited. If the bride-to-be in your life prefers a couple's shower, here's how to throw one.

1. BEND THE RULES. The best part about throwing a couple's shower is that since it's a newer concept, there really are no rules. Talk to the couple about the kind of party they'd like to have—brunch, dinner, cocktail party, you name it. Guests can bring gifts, but whether or not they are opened at the shower is up to the couple. Like a bridal shower, it should be held three weeks to three months before the wedding. Anyone can host the party—a family member, members of the wedding party, a close family friend. And it can be held anywhere they'd like, whether it's in the couple's backyard, their favorite restaurant, or a parent's home.

2. CREATE THE GUEST LIST. Everyone invited to a couple's shower should also be invited to the wedding. Ask the couple to provide you with the guest list; they should try to keep this party intimate and invite just their VIPs—wedding party members, both sets of parents, siblings, and close friends. Ideally, the shower should be smaller than an engagement party, with thirty guests or fewer.

3. CHOOSE A THEME. While it isn't necessary to have one, a shower theme will help guests figure out what type of gift to buy and bring to the celebration. If you decide to have a party theme, choose one that's based on something the couple enjoys doing together, such as traveling, camping, or cooking. Another idea: a "Stock the Bar" theme, where guests are encouraged to bring booze, barware, and cocktail recipe books to help the couple stock their at-home bar. If the couple is planning to make some renovations to their home, a "home improvement" theme might be fitting; guests can gift them with power tools, home decor, or items they may have registered for at a home-improvement store.

4. CONSIDER THE DETAILS. Put as much care and thought into a couple's shower as you would into a traditional bridal shower. If possible, have one member from each side of the wedding party take the lead in planning and hosting the party together, with assists from the rest of the attendants. Send invitations by snail mail or email six to eight weeks before the party date (make sure the wording on the invitation makes it clear to guests that it's a joint shower), order flower arrangements, create a menu that reflects both of their tastes, and decorate the space with string lights or candlelit lanterns to add a cozy ambiance.

5. PLAY GAMES. Showers typically involve some sort of game, so incorporate a game or two that pits the couple against each other and draws a lot of laughs. Find some ideas for shower games your guests will actually be excited to play on page 132.

6. HONOR THE COUPLE. Like a traditional shower, the point of the party is to honor the soon-to-be-wedded couple, so think about creative ways to celebrate them. Order a cake from their favorite bakery, serve pizza from their neighborhood joint, name the specialty cocktail after their dog, and invite guests to give a toast (or maybe an all-in-good-fun roast?).

Bridal shower themes

Although a theme isn't an absolute must for a bridal shower, having one will make party planning easier for the hosts. Plus, a well-thought-out party theme makes for a more memorable event for guests (trust me, the last thing you want is to throw a cookie-cutter bridal shower). When brainstorming potential themes, put yourself in the bride's shoes: What setting and aesthetic best fits her personality? What food and drinks would she love the most? What activities would the bride and her friends enjoy doing? Keep reading for some modern, not-lame shower themes to get you inspired.

#SELFCARESUNDAY

Help the bride relax before the big day with an afternoon of pampering and self-care. Hire a professional makeup artist to give a private lesson to all the guests, or look into local beauty-product boutiques where you can blend your own perfume or customize your own lipstick shade. Send guests home with goody bags filled with sheet masks, lip gloss, and nail polish.

GARDEN PARTY

If your bride has a green thumb, throw a shower with a nature-inspired theme. Hire a local florist to teach a beginner's flower-arranging or DIY flower-crown class, or have them create a "bouquet bar" where guests can make their own bouquet of flowers to wrap and bring home. Be sure to order a floral hair crown for the bride to wear during the party and include packets of wildflower seeds in favor bags so guests can create their own blooming garden at home. Other on-theme ideas: a succulent-potting party, DIY terrarium-making class, or a kokedama workshop (*kokedama* is a Japanese botanical art form involving potting plants in a ball of moss and displaying them suspended in the air).

WINE TASTING 101

Bridal showers and bubbly go hand in hand, but instead of the standard mimosas, invite a sommelier or wine expert to guide the group through the basics of how to taste and pair wines. Decorate the party space (the bride's favorite wine bar, perhaps?) with wine bottles filled with fresh flowers, and serve an array of small bites—each paired with a different wine—instead of a seated luncheon. Provide cute notecards so guests can jot down their tasting notes; before everyone departs, gift them with a bottle of the bride's favorite vino or bubbly to enjoy at home.

WRITTEN IN THE STARS

If your bride-to-be begins every morning with coffee and her horoscope, then an astrology-themed shower might be written in the stars. Kick off the party with readings from an astrologer, fortune-teller, or tarot card–reader—guests will become acquainted with each other quickly after learning about their horoscopes, futures, and intuitions. Decorate the party space with candlelit lanterns, kilim rugs, and plenty of comfy floor cushions, and give each guest a sage smudge stick or crystal to take home.

MOVEMENT AND MINDFULNESS

For a health-and-wellness-themed bridal shower, bring in an instructor to lead a vinyasa flow yoga class or guided meditation; afterward, guests can help themselves to healthy refreshments including cold-pressed juices, acai bowls, and a make-your-own smoothie bar with mix-ins like protein powder, bee pollen, and spirulina. Party favors could include roll-on essential oils and a chic reusable water bottle (you could even personalize the bottles, but do it in a way that's not just the bride's name and the shower date—guests are more likely to reuse something if the design is more general).

DESTINATION: HONEYMOON

If the couple has already booked their honeymoon, get the bride psyched for her upcoming trip by throwing a travel-themed bridal shower inspired by their destination. Design a menu featuring popular foods and drinks from the region, create a party soundtrack of travel-inspired tunes, and encourage guests to dress in destination-inspired attire (for example, Breton-striped shirts for a romantic trip to Paris, tropical prints for a honeymoon in Hawaii). Before guests depart, gift them with a themed favor, like a mini bottle of sunscreen and flip-flops, a personalized luggage tag, or a travel-size scented candle to bring on their next vacation.

BON APPÉTIT

For the bride-to-be who loves to cook, throw a culinary-themed shower so she can channel her inner Ina Garten and hone her skills in the kitchen. Bring your group to a local cooking school and learn how to master the bride's favorite dishes—anything from seafood paella and made-from-scratch pappardelle pasta to Shanghai soup dumplings and French macarons. The relaxed atmosphere and communal activity will help break the ice among guests; plus, the group will get to enjoy a delicious meal at the end of the class. As for shower gifts, ask guests to each share a favorite recipe on a notecard paired with a gift that will help the bride make the dish at home. For example, if someone shares their go-to chocolate-chip cookie recipe, they could also gift the bride a set of mixing bowls, a baking sheet, and a pair of their favorite spatulas.

KILN IT!

A private ceramics class is the perfect shower activity for DIY brides who love to roll up their sleeves and get their hands a little dirty. Book a beginner's class at a local pottery studio; everyone will learn how to throw a pot on a pottery wheel and create their own ceramic masterpiece. Bonus: A hands-on activity like pottery can be a great tension-reliever, so if your bride-to-be is feeling anxious before the wedding, this might be the perfect way to de-stress.

Bridal shower games and activities

Here's the thing about bridal shower games: We've seen most of them already. Yawn. The best games should get guests talking and toasting—not cringing and checking their phones. Below you'll find several creative ideas for games that all your guests will be excited to play.

This shower game tests how well the partners know each other and is a guaranteed good time. Before the bridal shower, email a list of questions to the bride's partner for them to answer. Aim for a mix of questions about the bride, about her partner, and about their relationship; keep the questions lighthearted and steer away from anything negative or too personal. At the bridal shower, ask the bride the same questions and see if her answers match her partner's. Make it even more interactive by video-calling her partner during the party and having them answer the questions live (project the video on a screen or TV, if you're able to). If you are throwing a couple's shower, this game is a must. It's a favorite for good reason—the game is always endearing and funny, and it helps everyone get to know them as a couple. Here are some sample questions to help get you started, but you should feel free to customize them to suit the couple.

133

Questions about the bride:

What's her favorite food?

What's her least favorite food?

Where would she go on vacation tomorrow, if money/weather were no object?

Which three things would she bring to a desert island?

What's her favorite movie?

What's her guilty pleasure?

What does your family love most about her?

Questions about the bride's partner:

What's the best meal you have cooked for her?

What's your most annoying habit?

Are you a morning person or a night owl?

What's your go-to drink?

What's your favorite book?

What's your irrational fear?

Which movie do you most quote from?

Questions about their relationship:

Where was your first date?	Who usually apologizes first after an argument?
Where was your first kiss?	What are your pet names for each other?
Where was your second date?	What's your favorite thing about her?
Who said "I love you" first?	

ADVICE FOR THE BRIDE

Set up a table at the shower and invite guests to offer the to-be-weds their best marriage advice. Put out pens and notecards that are preprinted with fill-in-the-blank prompts; guests can write their ideas on the cards and place them in a box or jar for the guest of honor to take home. Older guests with decades of marriage under their belts might want to share some words of wisdom and advice for a happy marriage, while younger guests can offer date-night ideas, such as local restaurants to check out, recipes to try, and movies to watch.

A SMASHING GOOD TIME

This one's guaranteed to be a hit. Order a wedding-themed piñata (for example, a piñata shaped like an engagement ring, wedding cake, or champagne bottle), and fill it with grown-up goodies, such as lottery scratchers, mini bottles of booze and wine (in plastic bottles and bubble-wrapped), $5 gift cards, candy, lip balm, ring pops, travel-size beauty products, face masks, and fizzy bath bombs. Each guest can take a turn whacking the piñata while blindfolded until it cracks open and the goodies spill out.

WHERE IN THE WORLD?

If the bride (or the couple) loves to travel, then this game is the perfect activity for their shower. Print out photos of the bride taken during different trips and vacations throughout her life (enlist help from her parents for a few childhood vacation pics). Display them in frames or on a clothesline with wooden pins; number each photo and have guests guess where the picture was taken. You could also add another element to the game by asking trivia questions about the locations; the guest with the most right answers wins a prize, such as a goody bag filled with travel-size toiletries and beauty products.

If many of the bride's family members will be in attendance, be sure to include this game in the mix because it just might turn into a sentimental walk down memory lane. Make a big collage of photos of the bride at various ages (again, you might need help from her parents to track down childhood photos); you could also frame them (the bride and family members could take them home afterward). Aim to get a good mix of adorable baby photos, awkward preteen class pictures, and photos from her college days dressed in outfits she'd probably rather forget. Number each photo and have shower guests guess the age she was in each picture. You could also ask attendees to bring a couple of photos of themselves taken with the lady of the hour. At the shower, pass out pens and paper, and have guests write captions for the pics and place the snapshots in an album. Pass the album around for everyone to look at, then give it to the bride as a keepsake.

Gift-opening alternatives

Some brides find the idea of opening gifts in front of their guests a little uncomfortable and would prefer to do it in private. If that sounds like your bride-to-be, here are some alternatives:

- Skip opening the gifts altogether. Forgo having the bride open presents in front of everyone, and use that time to hang out with guests instead.

- Ask guests to leave their gifts unwrapped. Include a line on the shower invitation requesting that guests bring unwrapped gifts. At the party, the bride can be there to greet guests as they arrive and accept gifts with a warm thanks; or, the unwrapped presents can be displayed on a table for the duration of the party (each present should be labeled with the gift-giver's name). This is also sometimes called a "display shower."

- Ask guests to wrap their gifts in clear cellophane. Some bridal shower invitations may request that gifts be "wrapped in clear," which typically means wrapping the present in cellophane instead of wrapping paper (using tulle also works). This way, everyone still gets a peek at the gift during the party.

TIMELINE: **Planning the bridal shower**

Planning the bridal shower (or couple's shower) is an all-hands-on-deck undertaking. The maid of honor/honor attendant traditionally takes the lead (even if someone else is hosting the bridal shower, like the bride's relatives), but all the bridal party members should take on responsibilities and tasks to collectively plan an amazing party for the bride-to-be. To help you stay on top of everything, from ordering invitations to assembling party favors, use the following timeline.

THREE OR MORE MONTHS BEFORE:

CONSULT WITH THE BRIDE. Before you start planning, talk to the bride to confirm that she would like to have a bridal shower. If she does, ask her (or the couple, if it's a joint party) about what she is envisioning. To help guide that conversation, have her fill out

The Bridal Shower: Setting Expectations worksheet on page 222. Gauge her comfort level with group activities like games and gifts (is she OK with opening gifts in front of everyone or would she prefer not to?), and talk about potential venues, bridal shower themes, and any ideas for the kind of celebration she would like (or wouldn't like). Use these insights to plan the party.

GET THE GUEST LIST AND GUESTS' CONTACT INFO. Ask the bride to provide you with a guest list, including email addresses, mailing addresses, and phone numbers.

PICK A DATE AND TIME. Have the bride provide a few options for dates and times that work for her; consult with important guests, such as the bridal party members and close family members, to pick a date that works best for everyone.

FIND A VENUE. Determine where to host the party, whether it's at a rented event space, a local restaurant or café, or someone's home or backyard. Make reservations, if needed.

SET A BUDGET AND STICK TO IT. If a friend or family member has offered to host the bridal shower, check in with the host to see how the bridal party members can help contribute, whether it's monetarily, helping prepare food, or decorating the space. If the bridal party members are hosting the shower, have a conversation with all the attendants about setting a reasonable budget that works for everyone. Consider the number of guests and the cost of the location, food, drinks, and any game prizes when determining the maximum amount you want to spend. Watch your spending carefully—you might have the urge to make the party look Pinterest-worthy, but all those pretty extras will add up fast.

DECIDE ON A PARTY THEME. Based on your conversation with the bride, choose a bridal shower theme that complements what she's envisioning.

ORDER INVITATIONS. Browse online stationery companies and choose an invitation design that complements the shower theme. Be sure to include the bride's name (or the couple's names, if it's a joint shower), date and time, location, registry information, the name(s) of the host(s), how to RSVP, and the RSVP deadline (the date should be two to four weeks before the party to give you enough time to finalize all the details). The invitation also should include any additional information about the shower, such as a dress code, gift-wrapping guidance, or anything the guest should bring (for example, photos or a favorite recipe to share with the guest of honor).

DELEGATE TASKS TO BRIDAL PARTY MEMBERS. Enlist the bridal party to help plan the decorations, games, activities, and menu. Delegate tasks like contacting vendors, creating a playlist, and bringing specific dishes.

HIRE A PHOTOGRAPHER. If you're thinking of hiring a professional photographer to document the party, book them as soon as you have decided on a date, as their schedules tend to fill up very quickly.

TWO MONTHS BEFORE:

SEND INVITATIONS. The invitations should be sent out six to eight weeks before the bridal shower, either by snail mail or email.

PLAN THE MENU AND ORDER FOOD. Figure out the menu; if you're ordering catering, select the caterer and book them for the party date.

DECIDE ON PARTY DECOR AND SHOP FOR DECORATIONS. Decide how you'd like to decorate the party space. Get help from the other bridal party members and DIY what you can, then purchase other decor items as needed.

ORDER PARTY FAVORS. Sending shower guests home with a small gift is a lovely gesture; choose a party favor that works with your theme and the group's budget.

PLACE RENTAL ORDERS. If you need to rent tables, chairs, linens, or equipment, place your order and schedule the delivery for the day before the party.

DECIDE WHICH ACTIVITIES AND GAMES TO PLAY. Work with the other attendants to figure out the entertainment and start prepping (buying supplies, preparing trivia questions, etc.).

ONE MONTH BEFORE:

ORDER THANK-YOU CARDS FOR THE BRIDE. Go the extra mile and order bridal shower thank-you cards for the bride so she doesn't have to. Give them to her at the end of the shower to help her get a head start on

writing them. Choose a design that matches the invitation; you'll get major extra-credit points if you order them preprinted with attendees' mailing addresses or if you handwrite the addresses yourself.

PURCHASE FOOD AND DRINK TABLEWARE. Assess what kind of tableware the host and bridal party members already own and can bring to the party, then order or borrow any additional items as needed (serving platters and serving spoons, beverage dispensers, cake stand, plates, cups, napkins, and utensils).

FOLLOW UP WITH EVERYONE. Check in with the host and bridal party members to make sure they're on track with their projects and tasks.

BUY A GIFT. Purchase the present you'd like to give or go in on a group gift with the other attendants.

TWO WEEKS BEFORE:

FINALIZE THE GUEST LIST. Everyone should have RSVP'd by now; follow up with anyone who has not responded via email or a quick phone call.

ORDER THE CAKE. Once the head count has been confirmed, order the cake or dessert.

ORDER THE FLOWERS. If you're hiring a florist, decide on the number of arrangements you'll need and place your order. Or, if you're planning to DIY the flowers yourselves, order loose stems from a local florist for pickup the day before the shower.

PICK UP ANY ITEMS YOU'RE BORROWING. Give yourself enough time to gather all the items you'll be borrowing so you're not rushed during the week of the shower (for example, serving platters, tableware, audio equipment, tables and chairs, and anything necessary for the games and activities).

MAKE A PLAYLIST. Put together a soundtrack to set the right party mood. Don't forget to bring a portable Bluetooth speaker to the shower!

MAKE A SHOPPING LIST. Create a list of all the food and drinks needed and delegate shopping for these items among everyone who's helping.

CHOOSE YOUR OUTFIT. Give yourself plenty of time to figure out what you're going to wear.

ONE WEEK BEFORE:

CONFIRM ALL VENDORS. Check in with all the vendors (party venue, photographer, caterer, baker, florist, rental company, and any other suppliers) to confirm all the details.

FINALIZE THE GAMES AND DECOR. Complete any DIY decor projects and make sure you have all the supplies and prizes for the games and activities.

ASSEMBLE THE PARTY FAVORS. Put together all the shower favors; box or bag them so that they're ready to be transported on the day of the shower.

PURCHASE FOOD AND DRINKS. If you're preparing food yourselves, purchase all the ingredients you'll need for the menu.

MAKE A FOOD-PREP SCHEDULE. Give yourself ample time to cook and prepare your dish(es).

FIGURE OUT THE ROOM LAYOUT. Visualize the party space and create a mental floor plan to facilitate decorating and setting up.

ONE DAY BEFORE:

PREPARE THE FOOD. Prepare any menu items you signed up to bring that can be made in advance (or do the prep work and finish cooking tomorrow).

CHECK IN WITH THE HOST AND OTHER BRIDAL PARTY MEMBERS. Touch base with everyone and confirm who's bringing what; also, be sure to ask the other attendants to arrive early to help.

SEND A REMINDER EMAIL TO GUESTS. Remind guests of the shower location and time, reiterating the address, and include your cell phone number in case a guest needs to reach you.

SET UP THE VENUE (IF POSSIBLE). If you're able to access the party venue ahead of time, arrange to be there to set up the tables and chairs, receive rental deliveries, and decorate.

PACK EVERYTHING YOU'LL NEED TO BRING. Box and bag everything you'll be bringing to the shower and put them by the front door so you don't forget anything. Place a sticky note on the front door listing any items in the refrigerator you'll need to bring.

RUN ANY LAST-MINUTE ERRANDS.

DAY OF:

PREPARE THE REMAINING DISHES. Finish making your menu items and pack them to transport to the shower.

PICK UP ANY ORDERED ITEMS. Pick up the flowers, cake/dessert, purchased food, and any other items that were ordered in advance.

ARRIVE EARLY. All the bridesmaids/attendants should arrive at the venue one or two hours early to set everything up.

DECORATE THE SPACE. Finish setting up and decorating the party space. Don't forget to put the champagne on ice!

WELCOME GUESTS AND HAVE FUN! Greet guests as they arrive, mingle with everyone, keep an eye on any refreshments that need refilling, run any games that are planned, and have a great time! And, of course, check on the bride to make sure she's got everything she needs.

OFFER A TOAST. This is optional, but if you'd like to say a few words to the bride-to-be, offer a toast during the meal (be sure to give the host a heads-up ahead of time).

HELP THE BRIDE OPEN HER GIFTS. When it's time to open the gifts, ask a few bridal party members to help streamline the process. Recruit one person for each of these tasks: passing gifts to the bride, making a list of who gave each present (so the bride can write her thank-you notes later), clearing the wrapping paper, and making a ribbon bouquet (more on that on page 153). Be sure to have these supplies on hand: scissors, paper and pen, trash bags (one for recycling, another for garbage), and sticky notes (to label any similar gifts and keep them organized). To keep track of gifts, make a copy of the guest list and leave space next to each name to jot down the gift they gave. Another method is to collect the cards attached to the gifts and write down the item given on the back of the card. Or, you could simply grab a pen and paper and make the gift list as the bride opens each present. At the end of the shower, give her the list, along with the thank-you cards you already ordered and addressed for her.

HELP THE BRIDE PACK THE CAR. After the guests have departed, help the bride bring the gifts to her vehicle and load the car.

Turn to chapter ten on page 238 for a handy reference version of this bridal shower timeline.

SAMPLE BRIDAL SHOWER SCHEDULE

Use this sample schedule as a template for your own party timeline.

12:30 P.M. *Guests arrive*

Guests mingle, enjoy a drink from a self-serve beverage station, and sign the guest book.

1:00 P.M. *Lunch*

The host welcomes everyone to the bridal shower and invites guests to take a seat and enjoy lunch.

1:30 P.M. *Toasts*

As guests are finishing lunch, invite them to give a brief toast. It's usually best to have planned the speeches ahead of time, but if the bride is comfortable with guests offering spur-of-the-moment toasts, then roll with it.

1:45 P.M. *Game #1*

A bridal party member can explain the rules before the game begins.

2:15 P.M. *Game #2*

Another bridal party member can explain the rules before the game begins.

2:45 P.M. *Dessert*

Serve cake or dessert; award prizes to the game winners.

3:00 P.M. *Gifts*

The bride opens gifts while guests enjoy dessert.

3:30 P.M. *Farewell*

As guests depart, give each attendee a small parting gift and thank them for coming.

How to Make a Rehearsal Ribbon Bouquet

A bride shouldn't walk down the aisle at the wedding rehearsal empty-handed. Instead, make a faux bouquet for her to hold, fashioned from ribbons from her bridal shower gifts.

To make a ribbon bouquet, use scissors to cut a ½-inch (12 mm) *X* in the center of a small paper plate. Fold each piece of ribbon in half, and make a knot in the middle of the folded ribbon. Thread the ribbon ends from the top down through the *X* until the knots rest on the surface of the plate. Once all the ribbons have been threaded through the plate, gather the ribbon ends together, and starting just below the plate, bind them together by wrapping them tightly with an additional ribbon to create a 4-inch (10 cm) handle. Secure the binding ribbon with two straight pins. Trim the ribbon ends to various lengths, then finish by cutting the ends at an angle or with notches.

CHAPTER SEVEN

How to Plan a Bachelorette Party

As the wedding day approaches, one of the remaining tasks on your to-do list is to throw your BFF a bachelorette party. Now, a basic bachelorette usually involves a night out to celebrate the bride-to-be, but a truly great one will have guests leaving with full hearts, lingering hangovers, and epic you-had-to-be-there stories that will become the stuff of legend. Are you ready? Here's everything you need to know to throw the bride her dream party (and stay sane while planning her big marriage send-off).

The bachelorette party: FAQs

Never planned a bachelorette party before and not sure where to start? Here's a rundown of the basics.

WHAT'S A BACHELORETTE PARTY? A bachelorette party is a rite of passage celebrating the bride-to-be's final days before she ties the knot and becomes a married lady. Traditionally, bachelorette party attendees were female-only; these days, modern brides really just want to party with their closest friends and family members, no matter their gender.

WHAT DO YOU USUALLY DO AT A BACHELOR-ETTE PARTY? Bachelorette parties used to consist of a wild and rowdy night on the town, just like you'd see in the movies: possibly a stripper or two, penis-shaped straws in a giant punch bowl of booze, and a beauty pageant sash bedazzled with "Bachelorette." Today, depending on the bride's preference, her bachelorette party might consist of an activity that jibes more with her personality and interests, whether it's relaxation (a pampering-themed trip to the spa), yummy food (a fancy tasting-menu meal at a Michelin-starred restaurant), or a good dose of vitamin D (a pool party at a boutique hotel). Then, there's the more-recent phenomenon of the destination bachelorette party, which is basically a group vacation to a far-flung locale, typically over a long weekend (more on this on page 171).

Find more creative bachelorette party themes on page 164.

Talk to the bride-to-be about what she's envisioning for her bachelorette and what her expectations are for the party. To help guide that conversation, have her fill out The Bachelorette Party: Setting Expectations worksheet on page 225, which outlines important questions about the party. And whatever she says, be sure to listen: If she says no strippers, that means no strippers!

WHO PLANS THE BACHELORETTE PARTY? The bridal party, led by the maid of honor/honor attendant, usually organizes and plans the bachelorette party. As with planning the bridal shower, it's important for whoever is in charge of planning the bachelorette to consult with the bride first—she should have a say in the overall party theme and style, as well as the activities.

WHO PAYS FOR THE BACHELORETTE PARTY?
Unlike the bridal shower, which is paid for by the host and bridal party, each bachelorette party attendee pays their own way. Usually, the guests pitch in to cover the bride's costs, as well as their own. However, if you're planning something more elaborate than a night out, such as a destination bachelorette party, then guests will typically chip in to cover an evening out rather than footing the bill for the entire weekend. However, some groups of friends have their own set of "house rules" when it comes to bachelorette parties. For example, a friend of mine has a close-knit group of girlfriends; for each

bachelorette party, they've collectively decided to cover all the bride's expenses, including airfare, accommodations, and all drinks, meals, and activities. So again, before you jump into party-planning mode, it's important to check with the bride first to get her input.

In addition to consulting with the bride, you'll also need to check in with the bachelorette party invitees to get a sense of what they feel comfortable spending. Be the liaison between the bride and her guests, and make decisions that work with the group's budget and reflect the style of party the bride would like to have. As party details begin to come together, let guests know what costs to expect, so they can decide if they're able to attend. Sketch out a preliminary itinerary with a tentative schedule, party locations, and estimated costs, and share those details with the group. Lastly, it's usually simplest to designate one person in the bridal party to be in charge of the finances for the whole bachelorette; that person should keep track of all expenses along the way and settle up with guests quickly post-party.

WHO'S INVITED? Ask the bride to provide you with an official guest list. She should feel free to invite anyone she'd like to have by her side to celebrate her last days as a single lady. The only rule is that all bachelorette party guests must also be invited to the wedding. The invitees might include her bridal party members, close pals (female or male) who are not in the wedding party, close relatives, and possibly her future sisters-in-law. Advise the bride to keep the guest list at twenty people or fewer, if possible (fewer than ten would be even better). Keeping the bachelorette party small will make planning less stressful and will also ensure everyone gets plenty of quality time with the bride-to-be.

WHEN SHOULD YOU HOLD THE BACHELORETTE PARTY? The bachelorette party is typically held anywhere between one to two months before the wedding date. The goal is to choose a date that's not so close to the wedding day that the bride will be stressed out, but not so far in advance that it will seem anticlimactic. Ask the bride to provide a few dates that work for her, then coordinate with the bridal party members to choose the best date that works for everyone.

In some cases, if the majority of bachelorette guests live far away, the simplest solution might be to hold both the bridal shower and bachelorette party on the same day or weekend (see page 119 for more on this topic). Or, you could hold the bachelorette a day or two before the wedding, when everyone is already in town for the celebration. (In that case, keep the festivities on the milder side to avoid hangovers and anyone feeling overly tired or worn down on the wedding day.)

WHEN SHOULD BACHELORETTE PARTY INVITATIONS BE SENT OUT? Formal bachelorette party invitations aren't always necessary; hosts can get the word out via email or a digital invitation website (like Paperless Post). Aim to send the invitations two months before the party (especially if you are planning a weekend-long event) to give people enough time to clear their schedules and make travel arrangements (if necessary). Stay on track with the bachelorette party planning by following the timelines on pages 170 (for a destination bachelorette) and 179 (if you're staying local).

WHO SHOULD SEND THE INVITATIONS?
Designate one person in the bridal party to be the point person responsible for communicating party information to all the guests. They can be in charge of sending the invitations, tracking RSVPs, and emailing the group as new details arise.

ARE YOU SUPPOSED TO BRING GIFTS TO A BACHELORETTE PARTY? No. Unlike a bridal shower, a bachelorette party generally doesn't involve presents, though someone might bring a gift for the bride to open during the festivities (typically sexy lingerie or booze-themed accessories like a tiny flask she can tuck into her purse).

163

ARE YOU SUPPOSED TO GIVE GUESTS PARTY FAVORS? Party favors aren't required, but if you have the budget for it, a small parting gift is a thoughtful memento. It could be something as simple as a reusable water bottle (for the inevitable hangover), some cheap sunglasses for a pool party, or a bottle of nail polish if the bachelorette is spa-themed.

IS THERE A DRESS CODE? Even though matching bachelorette outfits are all over Instagram, "Bride Squad" swimsuits and tank tops are never mandatory. If you think the bride will be into matching outfits, then go for it, but they're certainly not necessary. Remember that not everyone can afford one-time-wear bachelorette swag (and some guests might secretly be loath to wear it), so be sure to run the idea by the group before you go out and purchase a dozen embroidered jean jackets. However, if you still want everyone's outfits to be coordinated, a more wallet-friendly option is to suggest a broad clothing theme; that way, everyone can dig through their closet for something they already own. For example, if you're going to a pool and spa, suggest guests wear all-white cover-ups or floral sundresses.

Bachelorette party themes

There's no need to plan a wild, all-night escapade if the bride would really prefer something more low-key like relaxing at a lakeside cabin, taking a private cooking class, or road-tripping to wine country. If you're stumped for ideas, here are twenty-seven bachelorette party themes, from the classic dinner, drinks, and dancing to themes inspired by the bride's personality and interests, such as a guided distillery tour or an afternoon flower-arranging class. And when in doubt, run everything by the bride-to-be and make sure everyone's budget is taken into consideration. And most of all, have a ton of fun!

THE CLASSICS

- Dinner and drinks at her favorite restaurant, followed by dancing at the newest downtown hot spot.

- Front-row seats at a risqué revue.

- Book a private room at a karaoke bar, light up the disco ball, and keep the champagne flowing.

- Book a private class in pole dancing, burlesque, or aerial arts.

ARTS AND ENTERTAINMENT

- Visit a local historical site or museum for some education and culture. (True story: The last bachelorette party I attended included a tour of the local grain mill; I took home bags of fresh cornmeal as a souvenir. Nerdy, yes! But I loved it, and so did the bride.)

- Does the bride-to-be love the arts? Then she might appreciate a group outing (with everyone dressed to the nines) to the ballet, a classical concert, a musical, or the opera.

- Cheer on her favorite team at a local sporting event (and get her featured on the Jumbotron!).

LOTS OF LAUGHS

- Head to a stand-up comedy show; let the comedian know there's a bride-to-be in the audience, and prepare to be heckled!

- Get tickets to a local drag show and be sure to reserve tables near the stage.

SELF-CARE

- Plan a spa day for the bride-to-be with plenty of pampering, massages, facials, and spa water.

- Work up a sweat with a full-body group-workout class like spin, barre, or HIIT.

- If yoga is more her speed, book a private hot yoga or vinyasa class.

- Hire a teacher to lead everyone on a guided meditation and sound-bath session.

- Do a group cleanse by visiting an infrared sauna, taking turns in a sensory-deprivation float tank, or getting detox massages.

- Plan a pool party at a chic hotel, complete with fun floaties and frosty glasses of frosé.

THE GREAT OUTDOORS

- Head to the woods for grown-up summer camp (think zip lines, bunk beds, and trust falls).

- Lace up your sneakers for a scenic hike; be sure to bring some bottles of bubbly to open at the summit.

- Road trip to a local orchard to pick apples, cherries, or other in-season fruit.

- Go kayaking, canoeing, tubing, or stand-up paddle-boarding on a nearby lake or river.

- Charter a sailboat for a breezy afternoon on the water.

- If you'll be near a beach, sign everyone up for surfing lessons and learn how to hang ten.

BOOZING AND BONDING

- Book a private distillery tour followed by a guided whiskey-tasting session.

- Hire a pro chef to come to your place and do a hands-on cooking demo (then sample the results!).

- Climb aboard a wine train for an afternoon wine-tasting tour.

GET CREATIVE

- Learn to make a flower crown during a private flower-arranging class.

- Book a hands-on activity, such as an introductory ceramics or watercolor class (don't forget to BYO champagne!).

- Book a live model for a private drawing class.

What's a destination bachelorette party?

If your bride-to-be says she'd prefer to hop on a plane for a pre-wedding getaway instead of club-hopping downtown, then your next move is to plan an epic bachelorette party at the destination of her choice.

Planning an in-town bachelorette is already a big undertaking, but add to the mix plane flights, several days' worth of activities, and a gaggle of guests who perhaps have never met (and who now have to share bathrooms), and you've got yourself a major project to pull off. But with advance planning and some next-level organization, you'll be able to whisk the bride away on the destination soiree of her dreams. For guidance on the guest list and finances and everything in between, follow this planning timeline to successfully throw the ultimate bachelorette celebration away from home.

TIMELINE: **Planning a destination bachelorette party**

FOUR OR MORE MONTHS BEFORE:

CONSULT WITH THE BRIDE. Have a heart-to-heart discussion with the bride about what she wants (and doesn't want) for her destination bachelorette. To help guide that conversation, have her fill out The Bachelorette Party: Setting Expectations worksheet on page 225. Also ask these questions to help narrow down the options and pick the perfect location:

- What would you like the overall party vibe to be? Do you want a quiet girls' weekend or would you prefer a big-city bash?

- What's your preferred travel pace? Do you want a jam-packed itinerary or would you prefer lots of downtime by the pool?

- What locations do you have in mind? (Be sure to come ready with some ideas and suggestions.) Do you want to stay stateside? If so, perhaps New Orleans, Nashville, or New York City would fit the bill? Or are you itching to pull out your passport? Perhaps Tulum, San Juan, or the Bahamas are what you have in mind?

THREE MONTHS BEFORE:

GET THE GUEST LIST AND GUESTS' CONTACT INFO. Ask the bride to provide you with a guest list as well as the guests' email addresses, mailing addresses, and phone numbers.

CHOOSE THE LOCATION. When selecting the destination, take into consideration travel time, jet lag, and logistics. Although a weekend trip to Paris sounds incredible, is it worth spending eight hours or more on a plane? How about a city with European flair but is still in North America, like Montreal? If the bride's friends are scattered across the country, maybe you can meet somewhere in the middle, like Chicago. Are you an expert trip planner, or do you want to keep logistics to a minimum? Will an all-inclusive resort make sense, or do you prefer to set your own agenda and activities? Would she prefer to rent a private house and cook meals together? Be sure to also take note of average airfares and lodging costs as you're researching potential locations.

PICK A DATE. Have the bride suggest a few trip dates that work with her schedule, then check with the bridal party to pick the option that works best for everyone.

SEND A SAVE-THE-DATE EMAIL. Once the date(s) and destination have been decided, ask guests to save the date. Send an email to the invitees letting them know the party date(s), destination (including just the city is fine; you don't have to mention specific locations right now), and an estimated range of accommodation and activity costs based on your research (remember that some of the bride's portion will be split among the group). Encourage invitees to email you privately with any budget concerns.

SET A BUDGET THAT WORKS FOR EVERYONE. Based on guests' responses, set a reasonable budget for the trip—and stick to it. Be generous with any guests who aren't comfortable with the cost, and let them opt out of the activities without making them feel guilty. If possible, come up with ways to lessen the financial burden; maybe they can skip the spa treatment and hang out by the pool instead, or perhaps they'd like to stay for two nights instead of three.

SEND INVITATIONS. A bachelorette party is less formal than a bridal shower, which means you don't necessarily have to send out formal invitations—an email invitation or a digital invitation (like one from

Paperless Post) works well. Again, you don't have to have all the major details ironed out; a brief overview is fine at this point (include a line in the message explaining that you'll be sending periodic email updates as more details are finalized). Let guests know if there's a theme, dress code, or anything special they should bring for the guest of honor. Be sure to also share an updated breakdown of how much you expect everything will cost (per person) so everyone is on the same page. Give guests an RSVP deadline and list the contact person for RSVPs (with their phone number and/or email address).

CONFIRM COMMITMENTS BEFORE BOOKING LODGING. The last thing you want is for you (or someone else who's helping plan the party) to put down a deposit to reserve the accommodations only to have guests back out. Consider asking guests to pay a deposit to reserve their spot; this way, you'll likely see less fluctuation in the guest list, and the other guests won't end up having to contribute more money to make up for the guests who dropped out. (Note: Using a money-transferring app like Venmo or Paypal will make those payments quick and easy.)

BOOK LODGING AND FLIGHTS. Based on the group's budget, reserve the accommodations. You'll also want to make any flight reservations needed as soon as possible. Once you and the bride have booked your flights, send your itineraries to the guests so they can book the same flight or another flight that arrives around the same time. Urge guests to book their flights as quickly as possible to ensure availability and the best rates before prices begin to creep up.

TWO MONTHS BEFORE:

DIVVY UP RESPONSIBILITIES. The easiest way to make a bachelorette party a success is to delegate responsibilities to members of the bridal party as well as to other guests. Ask the bride's foodiest friend to make the restaurant reservations. Have a spreadsheet-savvy invitee create a detailed trip-planning spreadsheet and share it with guests (more on this below). If someone is a pro at accounting, put them in charge of handling the trip expenses.

CREATE A DETAILED ITINERARY. Create a shared trip-planning spreadsheet (I recommend Google Sheets) and ask guests to enter their flight arrival and departure times, along with the flight numbers—this way, you'll be prepared in case someone's flight is delayed. Create separate tabs for guests' contact info, expenses, local transportation, lodging (including the property's address and room assignments), meal-planning lists and restaurant reservations, a weekend itinerary, and a packing list (include attire notes for the weekend's events—from weather forecasts to club dress codes and necessary gear for outdoor activities).

ORDER BACHELORETTE PARTY SWAG. Purchase any goodies and swag you'll need for the festivities, including decorations if you're planning to decorate the bride-to-be's room, party props, and items needed for games. If you're planning on having guests wear matching bachelorette swag, order the items now to make sure everything arrives in time for the party.

ONE MONTH BEFORE:

CONFIRM THE GUEST LIST. Follow up with any guests who haven't RSVP'd to confirm whether they're able to attend. Email confirmed guests an updated itinerary as well as an updated breakdown of expenses.

ARRANGE LOCAL TRANSPORTATION. How will you get everyone to and from the airport? If most guests are travel pros, have everyone meet at the hotel or rental house. If they're nervous flyers, or if everyone is coming in on the same flight, consider arranging for a van to pick the group up and take you to your accommodations. Depending on the size of the group, you could book a couple of rental cars for the duration of the trip; or, you could hire a van to ferry the group from activity to activity. Be sure to also remember to arrange for rides (via a taxi service or ride-sharing app) if you will be drinking and venue-hopping.

PLAN THE MENU. If you're staying at an all-inclusive resort, food and drinks will be covered; but if you're renting a house and will be cooking some meals, plan for a big grocery run and determine which meals you'll need to shop for.

BOOK REMAINING RESERVATIONS. Book your tables at restaurants, clubs, and shows. Make spa reservations. Book group tours if you're visiting museums or other tourist attractions. Remember to negotiate for discounts or group rates (explain that it's for a bachelorette party).

ONE WEEK BEFORE:

FINALIZE THE ITINERARY. Email a final itinerary to the guests—be sure the shared spreadsheet is updated as well—that includes meet-up times, addresses of all key locations, and any other important trip details.

CONFIRM RESERVATIONS. Confirm your lodging reservation and make any necessary requests (for example, adjoining hotel rooms or specific tables at the restaurant). Confirm all other reservations and bring printouts of the confirmation emails, just in case.

CHECK IN WITH BRIDAL PARTY MEMBERS. Call each person in the party-planning crew to confirm their tasks and what they're bringing so nothing is overlooked.

START PACKING. Give yourself plenty of time to pack for the trip. Be sure to pack any bachelorette party swag you're bringing, such as decorations, props, favors, games, and signs.

ONE DAY BEFORE:

SEND A GROUP TEXT. Text the whole group a quick reminder about departure and meet-up details. Bonus: This way, everyone will also have each other's phone numbers.

CALL THE BRIDE. Check in with the bride to make sure she's got all the details and everything she needs for the trip.

CHECK IN FOR YOUR FLIGHT. Check in for your flight online so that you're not rushed at the airport the following day. (If you're road tripping, pick up the rental car.)

FINISH PACKING. Make sure you've got everything packed and ready to go.

DAY OF:

ARRIVE AT THE AIRPORT EARLY. Get to the airport early so you're not in a rush; keep tabs on everyone's flights so that you can track any delays.

WRANGLE EVERYONE UPON ARRIVAL AT THE DESTINATION. When you arrive at your destination, make sure everyone in the group is accounted for; next, organize transportation to get the group to your accommodations, if you are traveling together.

WELCOME GUESTS AND MINGLE. Once everyone's room assignments are sorted out, have everyone meet in the hotel bar (or in the kitchen of your rental house) for a glass of champagne. The hard part is over—now go mingle and have fun!

Turn to page 240 for a handy reference version of this timeline for planning a destination bachelorette party.

TIMELINE: **Planning a local bachelorette party**

If you're staying in town for the bachelorette, use this party-planning timeline so you don't miss a beat.

THREE OR MORE MONTHS BEFORE:

CONSULT WITH THE BRIDE. Before you start planning, ask the bride-to-be what she wants (and doesn't want) for her bachelorette. Maybe she'd like a girls' night out on the town, with dinner, drinks, and dancing?

Or would she prefer a spa getaway, with plenty of R&R? Have the guest of honor fill out The Bachelorette Party: Setting Expectations worksheet on page 225 and start planning from there.

GET THE GUEST LIST AND GUESTS' CONTACT INFO. Ask the bride to provide you with a guest list as well as the guests' email addresses and phone numbers (if you don't have them already).

PICK A DATE. Have the bride suggest a few dates that work with her schedule (and that ideally are one to two months before the wedding date); then check with the bridal party to pick a date that works best for everyone.

SEND A SAVE-THE-DATE EMAIL. Send an email to the invitees and let them know the bachelorette party date(s), location (including just the city is fine; you don't have to mention specific venues right now), and a rough estimate of what the costs might be (remember that the bride's portion will be split among the group). Encourage invitees to email you privately with any budget concerns.

SET A BUDGET. Based on guests' responses and their budgets, set a reasonable budget for the festivities (and stick to it).

DECIDE ON A PARTY THEME. Based on your conversation with the bride and her completed worksheet, choose a party theme that complements what she envisions.

DIVVY UP RESPONSIBILITIES. Enlist bridal party members and any additional willing helpers to pitch in. Potential tasks to delegate: contacting venues about availability and pricing, planning and buying decorations, organizing games and activities, planning the menu, creating a playlist, and buying and assembling party favors.

BOOK THE PARTY VENUE(S). After doing research, decide where to host the bachelorette. If you're making restaurant reservations, reserving private tables at a club, hiring an entertainer, ordering show tickets, or booking a group class, make the arrangements well in advance to avoid any last-minute hiccups in your plans. And don't be shy—ask if any group discounts are available.

TWO MONTHS BEFORE:

SEND INVITATIONS. A bachelorette party is less formal than a bridal shower, which means you don't necessarily have to send out formal invitations—an email invitation or a digital invitation works great. Again, you don't have to have all the major details ironed out; a brief overview is fine at this point (include a line in the message explaining that you'll be sending periodic email updates as more details are finalized). Let guests know if there's a theme, dress code, or anything special they should bring for the guest of honor. Be sure to also share an updated breakdown of how much you expect everything will cost (per person) so everyone is on the same page and there are no major surprises. Give guests an RSVP deadline and list the contact person for RSVPs (with their phone number and/or email address).

PLAN THE MENU AND ORDER FOOD. If you're going to a restaurant, reserve a large table or private room; if you're ordering catering, select the caterer and book them for the party date.

ORDER BACHELORETTE PARTY SWAG.
Determine how you'd like to decorate the party space. Get help from the other bridal party members and DIY what you can, then purchase other decor items and props as needed. If you're planning on having guests wear matching bachelorette swag, order the items now to make sure everything arrives in time for the party.

DECIDE WHICH ACTIVITIES AND GAMES TO PLAY. Make a list of the games you'll be playing and start prepping (buying supplies and preparing trivia questions, for example). Give yourself enough time to write out the rules and instructions (don't leave writing the game directions for when you're a few cocktails in!).

ONE MONTH BEFORE:

FOLLOW UP WITH EVERYONE. Check in with bridal party members and anyone else who is helping out to see if they're on track with their projects and tasks.

ORDER PARTY FAVORS. Sending attendees home with a small gift is a lovely gesture; choose a party favor that works with your theme and the group's budget.

ARRANGE TRANSPORTATION. Depending on the size of your group, you could book a couple of rental cars for the duration of the festivities; or, you could hire a van to take the group from activity to activity. Be sure to also remember to arrange for rides (via a taxi service or ride-sharing app) if you will be drinking and venue-hopping.

TWO WEEKS BEFORE:

CONFIRM THE GUEST LIST. Everyone should have RSVP'd by now; follow up with anyone who has not responded via email or a quick phone call.

CREATE AN ITINERARY. Plan a tentative schedule of events that outlines all the spots you'd like to hit, plus what time you want to get there. Double check to confirm all your reservations; don't forget to ask about drink specials, group deals, and bachelorette freebies.

CONFIRM RESERVATIONS. Check in with all venues and vendors (party venue, transportation, hotel, restaurant, etc.) to confirm your reservation.

CHOOSE YOUR OUTFIT. Give yourself plenty of time to decide what you're going to wear.

ONE WEEK BEFORE:

FINALIZE GAMES AND DECOR. Complete any DIY decoration projects and make sure you have all the supplies and prizes for the games and activities.

ASSEMBLE PARTY FAVORS. Put together all the favors, and box or bag them up to bring on the day of.

ONE DAY BEFORE:

CALL THE BRIDE. Give her a brief rundown of the schedule of events so she knows what to expect (but it's OK to keep some of the details a surprise!).

CHECK IN WITH BRIDAL PARTY MEMBERS. Touch base with everyone and confirm who's bringing what; also, be sure to ask the attendants to arrive early to help set up and decorate.

SEND A REMINDER EMAIL TO GUESTS. Remind guests of the meeting place and time, reiterating the address. If there are several stops planned, include the second address, too, for any latecomers.

PACK EVERYTHING YOU'LL NEED TO BRING.
Once you're all packed, set everything by the front door so you don't miss anything.

RUN ANY LAST-MINUTE ERRANDS.

DAY OF:

ARRIVE EARLY.

DECORATE THE SPACE. Finish setting up and decorating the party space.

WELCOME GUESTS AND MINGLE. Greet guests as they arrive, mingle, and have a great time!

Turn to page 241 for a handy reference version of this timeline for planning a local bachelor-ette party.

CHAPTER EIGHT

The Wedding Day: A Bridesmaid's Survival Guide

Whew, you made it! Your BFF's wedding day is right around the corner, which means you're in the home stretch (high five!). Quick reality check, though: The wedding is going to be a marathon of a day (you'll be on your feet for anywhere from sixteen to twenty hours), so you'll need to be prepared. This chapter covers everything you'll need to make it through the wedding day unscathed (and blister free!), from a hyper-detailed checklist of what to pack for the wedding weekend to a stress-free guide to acing your wedding toast.

What to pack for the wedding day

Give yourself plenty of time to pack everything you'll need for the wedding weekend. Start packing at least a week before the wedding: Grab the largest tote bag you own and begin filling it with everything on this packing list. And, if you're able, bring a few extras of some items; that way, you can hand out blister bandages and blotting papers to your fellow attendants to stash in their clutches (ensuring you'll be crowned the wedding day MVP).

THE ESSENTIALS

COPY OF THE WEDDING DAY TIMELINE. Before the wedding weekend kicks off, print any itineraries or wedding schedules the bride may have emailed to you. With these in hand, you'll know where you need to be and when to be there. Print a few extra copies in case someone in the wedding party forgets to bring their own.

WEDDING INVITATION. Tuck the invitation into your tote bag in case you need to reference important details like the ceremony time or the reception venue's address. Also, some wedding photographers like to shoot styled photos of the wedding stationery, so it's good to have a set just in case the bride forgets to pack one.

WEDDING PARTY'S CONTACT INFORMATION. Be sure you've saved all the wedding party members' cell phone numbers on your phone.

CELL PHONE CHARGER AND EXTERNAL BATTERY. You've got a long day ahead of you, so make sure your phone is fully juiced. Bring your wall charger as well as a backup battery in case an outlet is out of reach.

WATER. Don't forget to stay hydrated! Fill a reusable water bottle with water and ice, and keep reminding yourself to drink and refill throughout the day.

SNACKS. You'll likely be on the go for most of the morning and afternoon, without a moment to stop for a proper breakfast or lunch. Bring along a bunch of protein-rich, easy-to-eat snacks to keep your energy up.

SMALL PACKAGES OF TISSUES. Because there will definitely be (happy!) tears.

COPY OF YOUR SPEECH. If you'll be speaking during the wedding weekend—saying a few words at the rehearsal dinner, giving a reading during the ceremony, offering a toast at the reception—be sure to print out a couple copies of your speech.

WEDDING GIFT. If you haven't already mailed your wedding gift, make sure to pack it.

FASHION MUST-HAVES

REHEARSAL DINNER OUTFIT. Pack a cute outfit that will work for the ceremony rehearsal as well as the rehearsal dinner to follow.

WEDDING DAY OUTFIT. Place your bridesmaid dress/attendant outfit in a garment bag and hang it by the front door so you won't forget it.

TWO PAIRS OF SHOES. Bring the shoes you'll be wearing with your bridesmaid dress/attendant outfit and pack a second pair, as well—something comfier that you can change into toward the end of the night (flats, sandals, or cute sneakers are good options).

UNDERGARMENTS. Be sure to pack the right undergarments for the dress or outfit you'll be wearing.

PURSE OR CLUTCH. You'll need a small bag to hold your phone and a few essentials (like makeup and lip balm). Choose something small that won't be annoying to carry around all day.

JEWELRY AND ACCESSORIES. Tuck any jewelry you'll be wearing into a small pouch that you can store inside your tote bag until it's time to get dressed. Be sure to also pack a scarf or sweater to wear at night in case the temperature dips.

CLOTHES TO GET READY IN. Bring a set of comfy clothes to wear during the hair and makeup appointment, such as a pair of leggings and a button-down shirt. This way, once your hair and makeup are done, you'll be able to change easily without messing up your hairstyle.

ANOTHER CHANGE OF CLOTHES. If there's going to be an after-party, pack another more comfortable outfit to change into.

PORTABLE CLOTHING STEAMER. Skip the cumbersome iron and ironing board and get rid of clothing wrinkles in a flash with a handheld steamer.

DOUBLE-STICK FASHION TAPE. Because the last thing you want is a wardrobe malfunction right before it's your turn to walk down the aisle.

LINT ROLLER. A few minutes before the ceremony, give everyone's outfits a quick once-over with a lint roller.

SAFETY PINS. Buy a pack that comes with assorted sizes—use the mini-size pins to fix a small tear in a bridesmaid's dress (pin it on the underside of the fabric). Medium-size pins are great for reattaching a broken bra or dress strap. And if the wedding florist forgot to include boutonniere pins, you can save the day by using a large safety pin to secure the boutonniere to the suit lapel.

STAIN REMOVER. Spills are bound to happen, so be prepared with handy stain-remover pens or wipes.

MINI SEWING KIT. Look for a set that comes with a couple of needles, mini scissors, buttons, and thread in basic colors.

EXTRA TOTE BAG. Roll up an additional canvas tote and tuck it into your bag—you never know when you'll need an extra tote to lug stuff around.

BEAUTY MUST-HAVES

INSPIRATION PHOTOS. If you're getting your hair and makeup done, bring photos of the looks you love and want the stylist to replicate. Print out any inspiration pics or save them on your phone. Pro tip: Don't ask for a hairstyle or makeup look you've never tried before. Always ask for natural-looking makeup (unless the bride has super-specific requirements) and have your hair done in a way that feels comfortable.

YOUR OWN MAKEUP. Even if you're getting your makeup done by a professional, bring along your favorite makeup products to do your own touch-ups throughout the day.

SMALL MIRROR. If you're getting ready with the entire bridal party, the bathroom is going to get crowded. Bring your own mirror so you don't have to elbow in for room.

HAIRSTYLING TOOLS AND EXTENSION CORD. The hairstylist will bring her own tools, but pack a curling iron anyway in case the bride needs to touch up her hair before the reception. Also, bring an extension cord or surge protector, because there are never enough outlets for everyone's phone chargers and hair straighteners.

HAIR TIES AND BOBBY PINS. Pack a few hair ties to pull your hair back after working up a sweat on the dance floor, as well as extra bobby pins in case the bride's updo begins to come apart.

HAIRSPRAY AND MAKEUP-SETTING SPRAY. Make sure you and the bride look picture-perfect by giving yourselves a few spritzes of each throughout the day.

PERFUME. If you're planning to wear a fragrance, bring a rollerball of your perfume and tuck it into your purse.

DEODORANT. You'll be running around all day, so be sure to keep your deodorant nearby (make sure yours won't leave white marks on clothing).

BLOTTING SHEETS. Use these oil-blotting papers right before walking down the aisle to get rid of any shiny spots.

MAKEUP-REMOVER WIPES AND COTTON SWABS. Use them to quickly touch up any eyeliner or mascara smears.

NAIL POLISH, EMERY BOARDS, AND NAIL-POLISH REMOVER. Bring a bottle of your manicure shade to fix chips, along with a bottle of clear polish, which can be used in a pinch to stop a run in hosiery or glue a button that's about to fall off. Also pack nail-polish remover (wipes are best) and a nail file, just in case someone breaks a nail.

TWEEZERS. For any stray hairs and last-minute brow touch-ups.

MINTS. The last thing you want is for the wedding photographer to catch you mid-chomp on the gum you're chewing. Mints, always.

EXTRA-CREDIT POINTS

BOTTLE OF CHAMPAGNE. Coordinate with the other attendants to arrange who will bring the orange juice, champagne, and toasting flutes for wedding-morning mimosas.

STRAWS. Use them to sip water (or champagne) while you prep so that you don't mess up your lipstick.

MINI BLUETOOTH SPEAKER. You'll need this to play the getting-ready soundtrack you've been preparing.

A HANDWRITTEN NOTE. Give the bride the warm fuzzies with a handwritten card that expresses your heartfelt congratulations and well wishes for the future.

THE BRIDE'S FAVORITE SNACK. Surprise the bride with her favorite snack or candy, and make sure she eats something before the wedding.

Wedding emergency kit

In addition to the personal items (listed previously), bring some extra supplies to help smooth over any minor mishaps that might occur on the wedding day. This list may seem like overkill, but trust me, it's always better to be over- than underprepared.

Build the wedding emergency kit based on your own needs, the bride's needs, and her level of accident proneness, and store the items in a large pouch or tote bag (separate from your own packed items). Typically, the maid of honor/honor attendant puts the emergency kit together and keeps it nearby throughout the day. That way, if it's needed, it will be within easy reach, saving you from having to run a last-minute errand.

On the following pages, you'll find a list of everything you need to create a fully loaded wedding emergency kit.

HEALTH AND WELLNESS

- Toothbrush, toothpaste, and floss

- Eye drops (for allergies and redness; also consider eye-whitening drops, which will make your eyes look brighter and whiter in photos)

- Non-drowsy allergy meds (especially if the wedding is outdoors)

- Pain reliever

- Antacid medication

- First-aid cream

- Bandages

- Tampons and pads

FASHION AND BEAUTY

- Lotion (hand lotion and body moisturizer)

- Eyelash glue (if you'll be wearing faux lashes)

- Face-mist spray (for hydration and cooling)

- Nail clipper

- Brush and comb

- White chalk (to cover up wedding dress stains in a pinch)

- Extra earring backs

- Superglue

- Heel protectors (to keep your shoes from sinking into the grass)

- Spare underwear

FOOD AND BEVERAGES

- Granola bars/protein bars

- Candy

- Juice or energy drinks

LITTLE EXTRAS

- Jewelry cleaner (to make sure the bride's ring sparkles!)

- Cash

- Folding fan

- Compact umbrella

- Pen and paper (for writing last-minute notes and cards)

- Antibacterial wipes or gel

- Sunscreen

- Bug spray (especially if the wedding is outdoors)

- Lighter (to light candles or sparklers)

How to give the best wedding toast ever

Toasts are often the most memorable moments of a wedding reception, either for bringing roars of laughter and tears to guests' eyes, or for their cringey, epic fails. We've all seen toasts gone wrong: the maid of honor who rambles on making inside jokes that no one else gets, or the best man who turns his toast into a roast about the groom's drunken escapades and ex-girlfriends.

How do you avoid giving a lackluster wedding toast? It's simple: You need to be thoroughly prepared for your big moment at the microphone (and maybe save those

tequila shots for after your speech is over). Here's everything you need to know to deliver a wedding toast everyone (especially the bride) will love.

Wedding Toasts 101

The easiest way to start writing a great wedding toast is to put everything on paper first. Here's the basic framework for a successful wedding toast:

1. INTRODUCE YOURSELF. Chances are there are many guests in attendance who have no idea who you are. Begin your toast by briefly introducing yourself and explaining your relationship to the couple. Also, ask the bride ahead of time about the toasting order; if someone is giving a toast before you, consider how they might reference you and plan your introduction accordingly.

2. WEAVE IN PERSONAL STORIES. This should be the crux of your wedding toast—to share with the audience why the bride is your BFF and why the newlyweds make such a fantastic pair. Try to recall some of your favorite stories and firsthand experiences, and share them with the guests to bring these bonds to life. A classic wedding-speech anecdote is to recall a point in their relationship when the bride knew she had found *the one*. An epic toast I remember (now, more than a decade later!) involved the maid of honor digging through her email archives to unearth the message the bride had sent after the couple's first date. She hilariously read the bride's email out loud, which was giddy and gushy because she was completely smitten after date one.

3. CONGRATULATE THE NEWLYWEDS. This is a toast, after all, not just any old speech. End your toast by congratulating the couple on their union and inviting the audience to join you in raising a glass. Toast the newlyweds and their future together, then clink glasses with the couple and take a sip. Now, it's time to party (that tequila shot is waiting for you!).

Nine Tips for Giving a Killer Wedding Toast

Follow these steps to ensure you nail the delivery of this important speech.

1. GIVE YOURSELF ENOUGH TIME TO WRITE AND PREPARE. As soon as you are asked to give a toast, set aside time to brainstorm ideas and begin writing. Aim to start about two or three months before the wedding. Seriously, do not procrastinate or try to wing it—giving a toast is an honor and it's not something you should try to do off the cuff.

2. JUST START, ALREADY. Figuring out where to begin is the toughest part, so it's best to dive in. Start by making stream-of-consciousness notes; take a trip down memory lane and begin writing or typing all the stories that come to mind. Not every anecdote will be speech-worthy, but trust me, all of a sudden you'll land on a gem. Don't worry about editing at this point, just put everything down on paper; you can go back and choose the best details later. This will help you identify a theme, which is what you'll need to make your toast really memorable.

3. INCORPORATE A THEME. The key to a successful toast is to have a hook. Incorporate a theme at the beginning of the toast, and then return to it at the end. Having a solid theme will help tie your toast together, making it feel intentional instead of random. For my brother's wedding, I was his "best woman," and I began my toast by sharing how much that honor meant to me. Next, I told a few of my favorite stories about him and the countless times he'd been there for me. Then, to conclude, I addressed my new sister-in-law and explained that my brother had a proven track record of taking care of the important women in his life, and that he was forever going to be there for her, which made her—and not me—the real best woman of the night. Having that hook to come back to made the speech memorable and satisfying for people. (I still get compliments on that toast!)

4. **GIVE EACH PERSON EQUAL AIRTIME.** Even if you know one person better than the other, remember that you are celebrating the couple's relationship together—not your relationship with your best friend. Talk about the bride, but also find a way to include her new spouse. It's important to make sure your speech is well-rounded, because when it's not balanced, it's definitely noticeable to the guests.

5. **KEEP IT CLEAN-ISH.** As you're writing, keep in mind who your audience is. The guest list is probably comprised of multiple generations of your BFF's close family, friends, and even work colleagues. Although a kindhearted roast is perfectly fine, don't tell

any stories that may come across as inappropriate or that grandma might not want to hear. Steer clear of cursing, stories about exes, and any anecdotes that might shed a negative light on the bride or the couple. Keep the overall tone light and positive, and choose only the best stories to highlight the happy couple.

6. TIME IT RIGHT. Great toasts are usually two to three minutes long—enough time to share a few favorite memories and sentiments, but not so long that guests lose interest and zone out.

7. PRACTICE, PRACTICE, PRACTICE. Rehearse your speech several times before the big day to make sure you've got the timing down and that you've memorized the key points. Stand in front of a mirror and practice your toast out loud (not in your head). You could even use your cell phone to record yourself practicing—it might feel weird to watch yourself, but you'll be able to identify distracting mannerisms, such as verbal pauses like "um" and "like." With practice, you'll be able to hear any parts that might sound off and need revision, and you'll smooth out the rhythm and flow of your toast.

8. KEEP DRINKS TO A MINIMUM. A glass of bubbly before giving a toast can do wonders to take the edge off and loosen you up a bit. But try to stick to just one glass—too much booze can turn your carefully crafted sentiments into a big, slurred mess.

9. BE MINDFUL OF YOUR BODY LANGUAGE. A great toast isn't just about a clever compilation of words, it's also about the delivery. Before it's your turn to speak, take note of where the microphone is located; face the audience but also position yourself so that you're standing near the couple and can make eye contact with them. Stand up straight (always stand to give a toast; the couple will remain seated), hold the microphone with one hand and the printout of your speech in the other (double-spaced printouts or note cards are recommended; reading from your phone is trickier—you might scroll too fast and lose your place or it might turn off mid-speech and you'll have to fumble with your password). Try to avoid pacing, crossing your arms, tapping your foot, or any other nervous movements that guests might pick up on and notice. Hold the microphone close and speak louder than what feels natural—don't let all that hard work be for naught.

Start Brainstorming

To help get the creative juices flowing, ask yourself these questions as you're brain-storming ideas for your toast:

- Who is speaking before you? Consider how your intro will sound following their toast. You may want to make a reference to their toast or thank them for introducing you. Is anyone giving a speech after you? If so, you may want to introduce the next speaker at the end of your toast.

- What is the overall tone you're going for? Funny? Sentimental? Serious?

- Are there any specific themes in the couple's relationship or in the bride's life you want to highlight? What are some anecdotes that fit those themes and bring them to life?

- If you've known the bride since childhood, what memories stand out? Has she come a long way from the person you knew as a kid to the woman now making this commitment?

- How/when did you know the couple was meant to be?

- What's a favorite memory of the couple that instantly comes to mind?

- When you picture the couple's life together in a few years, what do you see?

- How will you wrap up your speech and invite everyone to join you in toasting the newlyweds? (Cheers? Please raise a glass . . . ? On that note . . . ?)

You got this!

The wedding day is right around the corner, and you're gonna be great. Here's my best advice, which I've saved for last: Book yourself a spa appointment for the day after the wedding. Because. You. Deserve. It.

Good luck at the wedding! She's seriously lucky to have you.

CHAPTER NINE

Setting Expectations

Since you are taking on a major commitment by being in the wedding party, it's important that the bride clearly communicates her expectations up front. I highly recommend talking with the bride about what she's envisioning from the get-go—this way, she won't be disappointed by any unmet expectations, and you won't be overly stressed out trying to make your own assumptions. To help facilitate this conversation with the bride, this chapter features four worksheets to guide a discussion about her expectations, one each for bridesmaid/attendant duties, maid of honor/honor attendant duties, the bridal shower, and the bachelorette party.

Give the bride a heads-up that you've found some wedding party worksheets and thought it might be helpful to go over them together. If she's game, send the worksheets to her ahead of time, then schedule a brunch date to go through her answers together over mimosas. This way, you'll be aligned on your bridal party role, duties, and what's expected of you.

BRIDESMAID DUTIES: SETTING EXPECTATIONS
worksheet

INSTRUCTIONS: If you've been asked to be a bridesmaid or wedding attendant, ask the bride to fill out this worksheet outlining what she'd like you to do and how she'd like you to help with the wedding planning process. Then, discuss her answers together. Preferably over cocktails.

I WOULD LOVE FOR MY BRIDESMAID/ATTENDANT TO . . .

BEFORE THE WEDDING	YES	NO
Help me shop for a wedding dress		
Attend wedding dress–fitting appointments		
Help with wedding planning tasks		
Help me shop for bridesmaid dresses/ bridal party attire		
Help plan the bridal shower		
Be a point person for guests who have questions about the wedding		
Help plan the bachelorette party		

	YES	NO
Attend as many pre-wedding events as possible, such as the engagement party, bridal shower, bachelorette party, ceremony rehearsal, and rehearsal dinner		
Give a toast at the rehearsal dinner		

Fill in the blank rows with anything else you'd like help with:

_____   _____

_____   _____

_____   _____

_____   _____

BEFORE AND DURING THE CEREMONY	YES	NO
Help keep me calm, fed, and hydrated		
Get prepped and dressed with me and the other bridal party members		
Walk down the aisle during the ceremony processional		
Stand by my side at the altar		
Walk up the aisle during the recessional, possibly paired with another wedding party member		

Fill in the blank rows with anything else you'd like help with:

_____   _____

_____   _____

_____   _____

_____   _____

AT THE RECEPTION	YES	NO
Mingle with guests		
Participate in the grand entrance		
Sit at the head table/your assigned table		
Assist with wedding dress adjustments and bathroom breaks		
Hit the dance floor and help get the party started		

Fill in the blank rows with anything else you'd like help with:

_____   _____

_____   _____

_____   _____

_____   _____

MAID OF HONOR DUTIES:
SETTING EXPECTATIONS
worksheet

INSTRUCTIONS: If you've been asked to be the maid of honor or honor attendant, ask the bride to fill out this worksheet outlining what she'd like you to do and how she'd like you to help with the wedding planning process. Then, discuss her answers together. Preferably over cocktails.

**I WOULD LOVE FOR MY MAID OF HONOR/
HONOR ATTENDANT TO . . .**

BEFORE THE WEDDING	YES	NO
Help me shop for a wedding dress		
Attend wedding dress–fitting appointments		
Help me shop for bridesmaid dresses/ bridal party attire		
Lead the bridal party (for example, make sure everyone has purchased their outfit and accessories, initiate planning the bridal shower and bachelorette party, etc.)		

	YES	NO
Help with wedding planning tasks		
Be a point person for guests who have questions about the wedding		
Plan the bridal shower		
Plan the bachelorette party		
Attend as many pre-wedding events as possible, such as the engagement party, bridal shower, bachelorette party, ceremony rehearsal, and rehearsal dinner		
Create an emergency kit for the wedding day		

Fill in the blank rows with anything else you'd like help with:

_____   _____

_____   _____

_____   _____

_____   _____

BEFORE AND DURING THE CEREMONY	YES	NO
Keep the bridal party on schedule		
Help keep me calm, fed, and hydrated		

Get prepped and dressed with me and the other bridal party members		
Make sure my wedding dress, train, and veil are perfect before I walk down the aisle		
Walk down the aisle before me during the ceremony processional		
Stand next to me at the altar		
Adjust my dress train at the altar		
Hold my partner's wedding ring during the ceremony		
Hold my bouquet during the vow and ring exchange		
Walk up the aisle during the recessional, possibly paired with another wedding party member		
Sign the marriage license		

Fill in the blank rows with anything else you'd like help with:

_____   _____

_____   _____

_____   _____

_____   _____

AT THE RECEPTION	YES	NO
Mingle with guests		
Participate in the grand entrance		
Sit at the head table/your assigned table		
Assist with wedding dress adjustments and bathroom breaks		
Give a toast during dinner		
Hit the dance floor and help get the party started		
Help with any last-minute details at the end of the reception (for example, distributing vendor gratuities, ensuring the wedding gifts are safely transported to their destination)		

Fill in the blank rows with anything else you'd like help with:

_____   _____

_____   _____

_____   _____

_____   _____

THE BRIDAL SHOWER: SETTING EXPECTATIONS
worksheet

INSTRUCTIONS: Before you start planning the bridal shower, check in with the bride about the type of bridal shower she wants. To help guide that conversation, set up a time to talk and have her fill out this worksheet to find out what her hopes and expectations are. Use her answers to throw an amazing bridal shower she'll remember forever.

THE BRIDAL SHOWER	YES	NO
Would you like to have a bridal shower?		
Or would you like to have a couple's shower?		
Would you like the shower to be a surprise?		
Would you like to be involved in planning the shower (if so, how involved would you like to be)?		
Would you like to play a few group games at the shower?		

THE BRIDAL SHOWER	YES	NO
What are some dates you're available?		
What are some times that work for you?		
Where would you like to have the shower?		
What gender makeup would you prefer for the party?		
Should kids be invited?		
Who are the VIP guests for the shower? (The hosts will make sure to choose a date that works for them.)		
Do you want to open gifts in front of guests at the shower?		

THE BRIDAL SHOWER

Do you have any particular shower themes in mind?

_____

_____

Are there any games or activities you'd like to include?

_____

_____

What would you like to have on the menu?

_____

_____

Are there any family members who might want to help?

_____

_____

Is there anything else you'd like the shower to include?

_____

_____

THE BACHELORETTE PARTY: SETTING EXPECTATIONS
worksheet

INSTRUCTIONS: At this point, we've reached peak party—the bachelorette is the final fête on your list of celebrations to plan. Ask the bride to fill out this worksheet to help give you some clarity on the type of bash she'd like, then use her responses to plan the best marriage sendoff ever for the bride-to-be.

THE BACHELORETTE PARTY	YES	NO
Would you like to have a bachelorette party?		
Would you like the bachelorette party to be a surprise?		
Would you like to be involved in planning the bachelorette party (if so, how involved would you like to be)?		
_____ _____		
Are classic bachelorette party props (tiaras, sashes, penis-shaped straws, etc.) OK, or would you prefer not to have them at the party?		

What are some dates you're available?

Do you prefer a small group or a larger group?

What gender makeup would you prefer for the party?

Who are the VIP guests for the bachelorette? (The party planners will make sure to choose a date that works for them.)

Do you have a specific venue or destination in mind?

Would you prefer a night on the town or a weekend getaway? Or something else entirely?

On a scale of one to ten, how wild of a party would you like?

What's your preference: for everyone to be able to attend or to celebrate at a luxe destination?

_____

Do you have any particular bachelorette themes in mind?

_____

_____

Do you have any specific activities and restaurants in mind?

_____

_____

Do you have a specific dress code in mind?

_____

Is there anything else you'd like the bachelorette party to include?

_____

CHAPTER TEN

Resource
Guide

Yes, it is possible to be an A+ wedding attendant without stressing out. In this chapter, you'll find the checklists, worksheets, and planning timelines we've discussed—all in one place.

Use them to stay organized, check off your to-do lists, stick to your budget, and basically totally ace being a bridesmaid.

CHECKLIST:

BRIDESMAID/WEDDING ATTENDANT DUTIES

Consider this your go-to, handy-dandy bridesmaid duties checklist for before, during, and after the wedding.

BEFORE THE WEDDING

☐ Be there for the bride.

☐ Be there for the maid of honor.

☐ Help with wedding planning tasks (within reason).

☐ Set a budget for yourself.

☐ Go wedding dress shopping with the bride.

☐ Help the bride shop for bridesmaid dresses/bridal party attire.

☐ Buy your bridesmaid dress/bridal party attire, shoes, and accessories on time.

☐ Spread the word about the couple's wedding registry.

☐ RSVP for the wedding and other events in a timely fashion.

☐ Book your travel and lodging.

☐ Help plan the bridal shower.

☐ Help plan the bachelorette party.

☐ Contribute financially to the parties (while staying within your budget).

☐ Attend as many pre-wedding events as possible.

☐ Buy a wedding gift.

☐ Give a toast at the rehearsal dinner.

GETTING READY AND PRE-CEREMONY

- ☐ Pack all your wedding day necessities.

- ☐ Arrive at the getting-ready location on time.

- ☐ Bring snacks!

- ☐ Help the bride get dressed.

AT THE CEREMONY

- ☐ Know your cues (when you're supposed to walk down the aisle and where to stand at the altar).

- ☐ Keep an eye on the kids in the wedding party.

- ☐ Walk down the aisle during the processional.

- ☐ Stand by the bride at the altar.

- ☐ Exit the ceremony during the recessional.

- ☐ Gather your and the bride's belongings and bring them to the reception.

AT THE RECEPTION

- ☐ Mingle with guests.

- ☐ Participate in the grand entrance.

- ☐ Sit at the head table/your assigned table.

- ☐ Assist with wedding dress adjustments and bathroom breaks.

- ☐ Hit the dance floor.

- ☐ Make sure the couple eats.

- ☐ Send off the newlyweds in style.

CHECKLIST:

MAID OF HONOR/HONOR ATTENDANT DUTIES

The list of maid of honor duties and responsibilities is pretty extensive. Find your inner person-in-charge and bring your organizational A-game to tackle everything on this list.

BEFORE THE WEDDING

- [ ] Be there for the bride.

- [ ] Lead the bridal party.

- [ ] Bring the bridal party together and help connect the group.

- [ ] Give everyone in the bridal party a say.

- [ ] Lean on your fellow bridesmaids for help.

- [ ] Help with wedding planning tasks (within reason).

- [ ] Discuss finances with the group and set a budget for yourself.

- [ ] Coordinate calendars with the bride and bridal party to choose the best dates for the bridal shower and bachelor- ette party.

- [ ] Go wedding dress shopping with the bride.

- [ ] Help the bride shop for bridesmaid dresses/bridal party attire.

- [ ] Buy your bridesmaid dress/bridal party attire, shoes, and accessories on time.

- [ ] Spread the word about the couple's wedding registry.

- [ ] RSVP for the wedding and other events in a timely fashion.

- [ ] Book your travel and lodging.

- [ ] Take the lead in planning the bridal shower.

- [ ] Take the lead in planning the bachelorette party.

- [ ] Find out what kind of party the bride really wants for her shower and bachelorette.

- [ ] Keep the peace among any conflicting personalities in the bridal party.

- [ ] Attend as many pre-wedding events as possible.

- [ ] Buy a wedding gift.

- [ ] Write your wedding toast.

- [ ] Create a wedding day emergency kit.

- [ ] Make a getting-ready playlist.

GETTING READY AND PRE-CEREMONY

- [ ] Pack all your wedding day necessities.

- [ ] Arrive at the getting-ready location on time.

- [ ] Bring snacks!

- [ ] Help the bride get dressed.

- [ ] Keep the bridal party on schedule.

AT THE CEREMONY

- [ ] Bring a few just-in-case tissues.

- [ ] Hold the wedding ring.

- [ ] Know your cues (when you're supposed to walk down the aisle and where to stand at the altar).

- [ ] Do a final wedding dress check for the bride before she walks down the aisle.

- [ ] Walk down the aisle during the processional.

- ☐ Stand next to the bride at the altar.

- ☐ Hold the bride's bouquet during the vow and ring exchange.

- ☐ Exit the ceremony during the recessional.

- ☐ Sign the marriage license.

- ☐ Gather your and the bride's belongings and bring them to the reception.

AT THE RECEPTION

- ☐ Help wrangle guests for group photos.

- ☐ Hold the bride's purse.

- ☐ Mingle with guests.

- ☐ Participate in the grand entrance.

- ☐ Sit at the head table/ your assigned table.

- ☐ Give a toast during dinner.

- ☐ Assist with wedding dress adjustments and bathroom breaks.

- ☐ Hit the dance floor.

- ☐ Keep an eye on the gifts and make sure they reach their destination at the end of the night.

- ☐ Distribute vendor gratuities.

- ☐ Send off the newlyweds in style.

WEDDING BUDGET
worksheet

Use this worksheet to figure out how much you
can afford to spend on wedding obligations,
keep track of purchases, and stay on budget.

YOUR WEDDING DAY LOOK	EXPECT TO PAY	ACTUAL COST
Bridesmaid dress/ attendant outfit	*$100–$300*	
Alterations	*$50–$200*	
Undergarments	*$25–$50*	
Shoes	*$50–$200*	
Accessories/ jewelry	*$50–$200*	
Hair/makeup/ manicure	*$100–$200*	
THE WEDDING DAY	EXPECT TO PAY	ACTUAL COST
Travel to the wedding	*$50–$1,000*	
Accommodations	*$0–$800*	

GIFTS	EXPECT TO PAY	ACTUAL COST
Engagement gift	$30–$75	
Bridal shower gift	$50–$100	
Wedding gift	$100–$300	
THE BRIDAL SHOWER	EXPECT TO PAY	ACTUAL COST
Travel to the shower	$0–$500	
Shower contribution	$50–$200	
THE BACHELORETTE PARTY	EXPECT TO PAY	ACTUAL COST
Travel to the bachelorette party	$0–$1,000	
Bachelorette party contribution	$50–$1,500	

TIMELINE:
Planning the bridal shower

Stay on top of everything, from ordering invitations to assembling party favors, by following this schedule.

THREE+ MONTHS BEFORE:

Consult with the bride about what she's envisioning for the shower.

Get the guest list and guests' contact info.

Pick a date and time.

Find a venue.

Set a budget and stick to it.

Decide on a party theme.

Order invitations.

Delegate tasks to bridal party members.

Hire a photographer.

TWO MONTHS BEFORE:

Send invitations.

Plan the menu and order food.

Decide on party decor and shop for decorations.

Order party favors.

Place rental orders.

Decide which activities and games to play.

ONE MONTH BEFORE:

Order thank-you cards for the bride.

Purchase food and drink tableware.

Follow up with everyone on their tasks and projects.

Buy a gift.

TWO WEEKS BEFORE:

Finalize the guest list.

Order the cake.

Order the flowers.

Pick up any items you're borrowing.

Make a playlist.

Make a shopping list.

Choose your outfit.

ONE WEEK BEFORE:

Confirm all vendors.

Finalize the games and decor.

Assemble the party favors.

Purchase food and drinks.

Make a food-prep schedule.

Figure out the room layout.

ONE DAY BEFORE:

Prepare the food.

Check in with the host and other bridal party members to make sure everything is on track.

Send a reminder email to guests.

Set up the venue (if possible).

Pack everything you'll need to bring.

Run any last-minute errands.

DAY OF:

Prepare the remaining dishes.

Pick up any ordered items.

Arrive early.

Decorate the space.

Welcome guests and have fun!

Offer a toast.

Help the bride open her gifts.

Make a ribbon bouquet for the bride to hold during the wedding rehearsal.

Help the bride pack the car.

TIMELINE: **Planning a destination bachelorette party**

Are you whisking the bride away for a bachelorette party bash at a dreamy destination? An out-of-town bachelorette is the ultimate pre-wedding escape, but it will require more managerial efficiency since there are additional travel logistics to consider. Stay on top of all the details—and stay sane!—by following this planning timeline.

FOUR+ MONTHS BEFORE:

Consult with the bride about what she's envisioning for her destination bachelorette.

THREE MONTHS BEFORE:

Get the guest list and guests' contact info.

Choose the location.

Pick a date.

Send a save-the-date email.

Set a budget that works for everyone.

Send invitations.

Confirm commitments before booking lodging.

Book lodging and flights.

TWO MONTHS BEFORE:

Divvy up responsibilities.

Create a detailed itinerary.

Order bachelorette party swag.

ONE MONTH BEFORE:

Confirm the guest list.

Arrange local transportation.

Plan the menu.

Book remaining reservations.

TIMELINE: Planning a local bachelorette party

If you're staying in town for the bachelorette, use this planning timeline so you don't miss a beat.

THREE+ MONTHS BEFORE:

Consult with the bride about what she's envisioning for her bachelorette party.

Get the guest list and guests' contact info.

Pick a date.

Send a save-the-date email.

Set a budget.

Decide on a party theme.

Divvy up responsibilities.

Book the party venue(s).

ONE WEEK BEFORE:

Finalize the itinerary.

Confirm reservations.

Check in with bridal party members on their tasks and projects.

Start packing.

ONE DAY BEFORE:

Send a group text reminding everyone about departure and meet-up details.

Call the bride to make sure she's all set and ready to party.

Check in for your flight.

Finish packing.

DAY OF:

Arrive at the airport early.

Wrangle everyone upon arrival at the destination.

Welcome guests and mingle.

TWO MONTHS BEFORE:

Send invitations.

Plan the menu and order food.

Order bachelorette party swag.

Decide which activities and games to play.

ONE MONTH BEFORE:

Follow up with everyone on their tasks and projects.

Order party favors.

Arrange transportation.

TWO WEEKS BEFORE:

Confirm the guest list.

Create an itinerary.

Confirm reservations.

Choose your outfit.

ONE WEEK BEFORE:

Finalize games and decor.

Assemble party favors.

ONE DAY BEFORE:

Call the bride and make sure she's all set.

Check in with bridal party members.

Send a reminder email to guests.

Pack everything you'll need to bring.

Run any last-minute errands.

DAY OF:

Arrive early.

Decorate the space.

Welcome guests and mingle.

What to pack for the wedding day

Give yourself plenty of time to pack everything you'll need for the wedding weekend. Start at least a week before the wedding: Grab the largest tote bag you own and begin filling it with everything on this list.

THE ESSENTIALS

Copy of the wedding day timeline

Wedding invitation

Wedding party's contact information

Cell phone charger and external battery

Water

Snacks

Small packages of tissues

Copy of your speech

Wedding gift

FASHION MUST-HAVES

Rehearsal dinner outfit

Wedding day outfit

Two pairs of shoes

Undergarments

Purse or clutch

Jewelry and accessories

Clothes to get ready in

Another change of clothes

Portable clothing steamer

Double-stick fashion tape

Lint roller

Safety pins

Stain remover

Mini sewing kit

Extra tote bag

BEAUTY MUST-HAVES

Hair and makeup inspiration photos

Your own makeup

Small mirror

Hairstyling tools and
extension cord

Hair ties and bobby pins

Hairspray and
makeup-setting spray

Perfume

Deodorant

Blotting sheets

Makeup-remover wipes and
cotton swabs

Nail polish, emery boards,
and nail-polish remover

Tweezers

Mints

EXTRA-CREDIT POINTS

Bottle of champagne

Straws

Mini Bluetooth speaker

A handwritten note to
the bride

The bride's favorite snack

Wedding emergency kit

Be prepared for anything
unexpected by packing
a wedding emergency
kit stocked with all the
essentials.

HEALTH AND WELLNESS

Toothbrush, toothpaste,
and floss

Eye drops

Non-drowsy allergy meds

Pain reliever

Antacid medication

First-aid cream

Bandages

Tampons and pads

FASHION AND BEAUTY

Lotion

Eyelash glue

Face-mist spray

Nail clipper   Bug spray

Brush and comb   Lighter

White chalk

Extra earring backs

Superglue

Heel protectors

Spare underwear

Granola bars/protein bars

Candy

Juice or energy drinks

Jewelry cleaner

Cash

Folding fan

Compact umbrella

Pen and paper

Antibacterial wipes or gel

Sunscreen

Acknowledgments

Thank you to family: my mom, brother, and sister-in-law, who always, without fail, have my back. I am so lucky to have the best team in my corner. Thank you to Bryce, who shows me what love looks like every day. Probably the best thing I've ever done was to swipe right.

Thank you to the team at Chronicle Books, especially to Christina Loff, for making the introduction, and Dena Rayess, for being an endlessly patient and thoughtful editor.

Strangely enough, I owe a debt of gratitude to the coronavirus pandemic of 2020. Through the crisis and chaos that ensued, it bestowed an unexpected gift: a rare expanse of time and quiet while sheltering in place, which gave me the space to write this book. I will never forget this weird, eventful year.

And, finally, thank you to the brides and the groom who have included me in their wedding parties. After writing about weddings for more than a decade, I've heard many not-so-great bridesmaid stories. But I don't have a single one of my own to tell, because I have been blessed with wonderful, kindhearted friends who have only embodied love and generosity on their wedding days. I am honored to have stood by your sides.